Love, Lutefisk, and Lemon Zest Sneakers

Patsy Baldus

Designed and produced by:
Maine Authors Publishing
12 High Street, Thomaston, Maine
www.maineauthorspublishing.com

Printed in the United States of America

To my Grandmother, " Bine":
You inspired me to write and to see the whimsy of the world.
Best of all, your cookie jar was always full.

Table of Contents

Beginnings 1
    The *Perkinsville Gazette* 3
    Banana Boats 7
    Steppin' Out 11
    Can You Come Out to Play? 15

Family Ties **27**
    Katy-Did. 29
    Boat Launch 37
    Can You Dig It? 41
    Up at the Cabin 47

On Vacation **57**
    Minnesota Madness 59
    Beware of Grizzlies and RVs 69
    Geckoes in Mexico 73
    Badlands/Good Times. 79
    Ride, Sally, Ride 85

Vets, Vignettes, and Doggie Treats **95**
    Willie Wonder-Boy 97
    Hind-Sight 103
    Deirdre, the Dog-Walker. 109
    Double Take 117

Face of Crimson **121**
    Just Warming Up 123
    Shake It, Baby! 127
    When One Door Closes... 133
    One-Stop Shop 135

Pause a Moment **141**
    Daylight 143
    Makin' the Move. 147
    Flower Fairy 157
    The Story. 161

Beginnings

The *Perkinsville Gazette*

Southern suburbia in the sixties was fraught with its own set of problems: segregation in schools and in local neighborhoods, materialistic desires to keep up with the Joneses, and how the suburban housewife could keep herself busy all day. At the tender age of ten, all I cared about was the fact that I finally lived in a neighborhood chock-full of kids! My family had moved from a remote farm along the James River on the outskirts of Richmond straight into nirvana, a suburb known as Varina in Henrico County, Virginia. Not that River Bend, as it was called, hadn't been a happy place for me—it was there that the seeds of my imagination had taken hold. Being an only child for ten years and having few kids around to call playmates had opened up a whole world for me—a world I created from this magical place along the river.

I brought this magic with me when I landed on Dan Street. This new world was laden with neatly bricked cookie-cutter houses, many of which were one-story ranches. And there were three blocks of these houses just bursting with the promise of kids. The three-block unit was called Perkinsville after old lady Perkins, who lived at the end of the first block. Her family had lived and owned land there for years. She was known around the blocks as the Queen of Homemade Cookies, which she dispensed freely to the kids who visited her in the summer.

I was euphoric living on Dan Street. Nothing made me happier than another neighborhood kid knocking on our door on a summer morning and asking my mom if I could come out and play. I explored every inch of those three blocks, met every kid possible who lived there, and quickly made friends with the Mills sisters, who lived about six houses from me. One was a year younger than me, the other a year older. It was destiny. I fit comfortably right in between them. Judy, the oldest at the ripe age of eleven (which she constantly pointed out to us) loved history. She had scrapbooks on John F. Kennedy, could spout facts and dates on demand, and loved to write. This was our connection to each other. I had written everything from horror stories (influenced by my secretly watching *Shock!* on TV) to poems about my dogs, to stories on the two black snakes that hung from a cherry tree at River Bend. Jane, the younger sister, did not share this bond with us. She only tagged along when she thought something exciting might happen.

It was natural for Judy and me to spend time sharing our stories with each other. We would sometimes find ourselves under the giant magnolia tree in Mrs. Perkins's yard, munching on cookies and dreaming aloud about Mike, a guy down the street who was gorgeous and only six years older than us. Judy always pointed out that Mike would undoubtedly go for her since she was the older and more mature person. Normally, that would start a mini war between us, but on this day, I had other ideas: Why not start a newspaper about the goings-on in the neighborhood? Judy forgot all about her plans for marrying Mike and was immediately excited about the idea. Her mom, who was an active member of the Laurel Hill Methodist Church, was the secretary there and had access to a mimeograph machine. She could make copies of the newspaper for us! We could sell this newspaper for ten cents to help pay for the paper. The *Perkinsville Gazette* was born!

Oh, and we had so many stories to tell! Like the time I innocently catapulted a girl named Cindy off my feet as we horsed around in the yard only to hear a loud *CRACK!* as she landed in a very unnatural way on her left arm. (Yes, it was broken!) Or how about the time Judy was learning to jump on the pogo stick and pogoed right into the doggie-doo in the yard... And then there was Carl—the heartthrob of my fourth-grade class who lived two blocks over... The romantic image of

Judy, he, and I dancing our interpretation of *Swan Lake* on the lawn one summer evening by candlelight would certainly make news…and it would offset his other image as the most relentless nose-picker in the class—but that was school, and this was The Neighborhood, and we were all about the business of Perkinsville events.

Our biggest topic for the newspaper, though, was Corinne L. She was my age and lived in the two-story brick palace at the end of my street. We all hated her with a passion. She had everything—a treehouse, long wavy hair, and most importantly, a Spyder bike, complete with a hot purple banana seat and a cute little white basket to hold all her jack rocks. Jack rocks, or "ball 'n jacks," was *the* entertainment for us kids. Hot summer days were spent on cool back porches. The scraping sound of those pointy little jacks when you bounced the ball and tried to pick them up without touching others evolved into fierce competitions in our neighborhood. Of course, we had to report the winnings to the *Gazette* to give credit where credit was due; but no, it wasn't Corinne who won these tournaments, but rather a sweet little redhead named Terry, who was a mere third grader.

Judy and I continued to plan and write the stories of our neighborhood in hopes of finishing up in a week. As I was working one day on a story about a nasty little boy named Sammy who regularly tortured his dog, there was a knock on our door. Judy's mom, Mrs. Mills (Edna) had come for a visit. She and my mom were best friends. I listened from upstairs in my room as they sat down with some iced tea and chatted. I overheard them giggling about our "cute idea" for a newspaper. I couldn't help smiling, but in the next moment, my heart sank. My mother had lowered her voice and confided to Edna that she thought she might be pregnant. Pregnant? I was old enough to understand what that was, and I was dumbfounded. For the past ten years, I had been entertaining myself and my parents. Now it would all change. I crept out of the house, hopped on my bike, and flew up to Judy's to spill my guts.

She didn't have much sympathy. "I live with Jane, remember?" she said. I was deflated but went back to work on my Sammy article for the *Perkinsville Gazette*.

A week later our paper was ready—hot off the Laurel Hill Methodist press! Judy and I had logged hours on our clanky bikes going around the neighborhood the previous week to pitch the paper and take inventory of who our potential ten-cent customers would be. We were pleasantly surprised when the majority of the neighborhood dropped a dime in our tin cookie can. Even Mrs. Mills was surprised that she would have to run fifty copies of the paper!

Judy and I had agreed to get up at six a.m. to divide up the papers and distribute them to the neighborhood, so people could enjoy our stories with their morning coffee. Listening to early-morning katydids hum their warning of the day's heat, we dutifully pedaled our precious newspaper around the three blocks. We finished in about an hour, nodded to each other sleepily, and headed home to crawl back into bed.

It didn't take long for the phone to start ringing.

I was half asleep but kept waking up each time the phone rang. With the umpteenth ring, my mother appeared in my doorway.

"Patsy, get up. We need to talk."

The look on her face said it all. There was trouble brewing in Perkinsville. Apparently, Perkinsville had been highly entertained by Judy's and my stories. In fact, no one was angry or upset. They were merely calling to congratulate my mother on her pregnancy. The last call had been from my dad at work. He had just gotten a call from a neighbor congratulating him on being a daddy for a second time. The problem was that my mother had not told him the news yet. She was waiting for a call from the doctor to confirm it...

Today the *Perkinsville Gazette* is carefully preserved in one of Judy's historical scrapbooks. It has been likened to a secret document in the Library of Congress. We have both grown and gone our separate ways, but still maintain contact even after fifty-plus years. The Golden Edition of that *Perkinsville Gazette* still binds us together.

Banana Boats

Entering middle school is hard enough for a sixth grader. Think back to those exciting, confused, chaotic, hormonal years. Now add in a size eleven foot and a height of five feet seven inches at age twelve, and then you really have something to talk about. You know, if I had been a tall, *graceful* girl, I could have handled the size of my feet. But I was busy dealing with other things like developing boobs (where did those come from?), gangly legs and arms, a monthly zit that appeared out of nowhere (yes, just one zit, but it was usually the size of Mt. Everest and positioned right in the center of my nose or lip), and something unexplainable that made me want to kiss the boy next door (he was a year younger, but that didn't matter). I remember my shoes always hurting because my toes (which were at least two inches long) were constantly growing—or at least it seemed like it. I loved the summer months because I could finally go barefoot and let those "big girls" go free. Sandals were like a gift from God—no confinement, and I could wear a size 10 since the toes were open.

Winter, of course, was a different matter. When I was a young girl, they simply didn't make women's, much less girls', boots in an 11. Of course, my mother, who was more frustrated than sympathetic, did what any good mother would do to provide warmth for her child's feet: She went to the men's shoe department. It was there I received my first all-black, rubber buckle-up men's boots. It took me a half hour just to get them buckled up, and by then I was sweaty, which is an ongoing middle school problem anyway. I was mortified to wear them and refused to wear them to school but wearing them outside to play with the neighborhood kids was OK; no one noticed or cared. They just wanted to get outside in the snow and sled down the nearby hill.

The spring of my sixth-grade year was the high point of my feet crisis. It wasn't quite warm enough for sandals, which left only one other alternative: sneakers. One day when I came home from school, my mother presented me with a gift. When I opened the box (it was a very long box), I was nearly blinded by the color of my new sneakers. They were what I would call *Lemon Zest* yellow. There was nothing shy about them. Did they fit? Well, of course they did. They fit perfectly. But you know how dark colors make things recede or look smaller and light (or should I say, BOLD) colors make things look larger? Well, you get the picture. It was like walking in giant banana boats. I had the feeling that my toes arrived way before the rest of my feet did. I can vividly picture myself walking across the schoolyard the next day to meet my class outside (I had been hiding out in the bathroom most of the day). They were in the middle of a science experiment. The wind had picked up. I was wearing a paisley tent dress that my mom had thoughtfully made for me to hide my hormonal chubbiness, and the dress billowed out in the wind. As the kids looked up, they must have thought a new-wave parachute with clown feet had just landed. I wanted to die. I made a mental note to myself: My next school science project should definitely be on *How to Stunt Metatarsal Growth.*

Somehow, I survived that day and went on with my life. There was one hiccup in high school when I needed a pair of saddle shoes for my one-year stint as a cheerleader. (Really, it was a dare...) I finally found a pair in the back of a large department store, or I should say, the clerk found a pair after digging around in the storage shelves. I proved that even size 11's could leap into the air with a *little* grace, anyway.

Later that year, a shoe catalog that must have been sent inadvertently to my house arrived in the mail. I pored over it. Jackpot! *Every* pair of shoes came in size 11 or the unthinkable 12's. Of course, many of the shoes were what you might call *serviceable*; that is, they were "Nana shoes"—black hard shoes that tied and were perfect for anyone ninety and older. Other shoes were white and thick-soled—ideal for nurses, I guessed. I nearly gave up as I turned the pages, but then I spied them: They were an anomaly for sure, at least in this catalog. *They were red.* Not just any red. They were fire-engine red. They were the most beautiful things I had ever seen! And they were stylish—Mary-Janes with a sexy T-strap and a blocky three-inch heel. I wanted them. I coveted them. And in that instant, I knew I had to have them for the upcoming spring dance at school. I could scrape together just enough money from my weekend job at the drugstore to order them. My mother didn't seem surprised when I showed her the picture in the catalog. She just smiled and hugged me.

Two weeks later, when the long, large box arrived, I slid those shoes on and pranced around the house like a newborn diva. My mother surprised me with a new dress she had sewn for me—white dotted swiss with tiny fire-engine-red flowers embroidered all over it. She had remembered from my dancing in her flamenco-style petticoat when I was younger that I would need a "costume" to complete my outfit for the school dance. From that moment on, I felt beautiful, regardless of my big feet.

As time went by, I worried less and less about my feet and concentrated on the more important parts of life: family and career. As I evolved as a teacher and a mom, so did shoe sizes. Size 11 was plentiful everywhere—online and in many department stores. Not surprisingly, my kids also have big feet; my daughter wears a size 11, which she carries off beautifully at five feet ten inches tall. And my son? He wears a size 15. Not a problem—he's in the same shoe league as the pro basketball players you see on TV. My sister wears an 11, and my brother wears a 14. My mother also wore size 11. Only now do I wonder and marvel that she grew up in an earlier time, unscathed by the plague of big feet. At least she never let on.

• • •

Foot trauma became pretty much nonexistent in my life until, at age fifty-two, I decided to try out Irish step dancing. I had always loved to dance freestyle, but this type of dancing was highly structured and one in which your arms stayed pinned to your sides. Eager to try something totally new, and being of Irish heritage, I thought I was the perfect student for this new adventure.

At the first class, our teacher announced what we would need for the class: loose clothing to allow movement and two types of special shoes—the *ghillie*, a soft leather shoe with laces along the instep and no tongue, and a hard, blocky shoe that looked a lot like the Nana-shoes I had seen in that catalog long ago. I could feel the panic rising in my throat. I knew I had conquered the *everyday* shoe dilemma, but here was a class with *specialized* shoes. A vision of long-haired young Irish girls with petite feet came to mind, jumping nimbly across the stage. The paisley tent dress and yellow sneaker combo danced into my brain all over again.

After class, I shyly approached the dance teacher. "Do they make those shoes you want us to get in larger sizes?" I asked.

The teacher immediately looked down at my feet and laughed. "Of course, they do. Women of all shoe sizes and shapes have learned to Irish step dance. Just go online to order them." Ah, life was good. I smiled in relief and turned to go through the door, nearly tripping on my own feet. That won't happen with the right shoes, I thought.

Recently, I purchased four pairs of shoes at one store, which seemed greedy and overly indulgent. But they were a great price, were everything from casual to dressy, and they all fit! At the checkout, I pretended to lament my indulgence. The clerk, a tall young girl, smiled at me. "Are you kidding?" she said. "I wear a size twelve shoe. When I find a pair that fits, I buy them! I had to wear ugly sneakers most of my life until recently."

I smiled. I suddenly understood how lucky I had been growing up, banana boats and all.

Steppin' Out

In fifth grade, I was already familiar with classical music. My family loved music, and they loved to sing. It was a natural progression on the musical spectrum to learn about the classics. My uncle, Skip, in particular, exposed me to the music of Verdi, Mozart, Beethoven, Tchaikovsky, and even Wagner. My parents had ordered the whole record collection of these famous composers through the *Reader's Digest*. Skip, who lived with us for a while, frequently borrowed their extensive collection for his own listening enjoyment. He would sit in his darkened room, classical music blasting. This was quite a contrast to the popular music of the time like the Beatles. I loved them, too, but the classics stayed with me simply because my uncle encouraged me to dance to them. He would shout out things like, "Dance! Dance! Dance the way the music makes you feel!" I would obey by flinging myself around the room, twirling wildly or leaping into the air in a very awkward arabesque. This was pure interpretation on my part since I had not attended one dance class. Skip would smile, satisfied that I had explored my inner expressiveness.

Sometimes the dance interpretation took place in the yard at our home along the James River. Uncle Skip would crank the music full blast out his bedroom window. My instructions were to feel the music and gyrate accordingly. Our yard was huge and sprawling, with open grass and several large sycamore trees. During my dance routines, I quickly learned to avoid the spiky seed balls these trees dropped. It was only natural that I needed a costume to go along with the music. I begged my mother to let me wear her petticoat—which was reminiscent of the 1800s. This petticoat was special: It had layers of tulle in rainbow colors. She finally relented when I begged her for the hundredth time. She was quite amused at my yard dancing and must have known I needed the petticoat to complete my look. I was in heaven. I had absolutely no inhibitions when it came to this. Music moved my soul.

It was no surprise, then, that I decided to join the band in fifth grade. And which instrument did I pick? Why, the biggest, brassiest, shiniest one on the table in the school gym: the French horn. I would learn to play the classics on my brand-new instrument. I was thrilled with my choice—until I had to pack it in the case and carry it back to the classroom. It weighed a ton! It also took up a lot of space by my desk. My classmates shot annoyed looks at me as they tried to navigate around it on their way to the front of the room.

Undaunted, I lugged it home on the bus that day, carrying the horn in my right hand and a pile of books in my left. Getting on the bus was an ordeal, but I managed. My parents were shocked when they saw the giant instrument parked in the dooryard. I had to run back to pick up my books, which lay in a scattered pile in the street. Balancing everything had proved too difficult, but I didn't want to admit how cumbersome this instrument was. My parents were willing to give it a go. I heard words like *practice, keep up with your homework,* and more *practice.* And practice I did.

My first band lesson at school consisted of learning to make noise come out of the instrument. This required blowing with your lips together to make a buzzy sound, which sounded more like farting to me. I did my best. Tighter lips plus pushing down one of the three valves made higher notes, and loose lips made lower notes. It seemed unpleasant and mysterious to me. The band instructor seemed much more focused on the dainty little flute players, not the only French horn girl in town. I felt abandoned. I continued to lug the instrument home and make buzzy noises with my lips. I really didn't know what I was supposed to do.

Steppin' Out

One morning several weeks after I had acquired the instrument, I was late getting up and getting ready for school. I grabbed some clothes from my drawer and threw on a gray wool skirt. The day was uneventful except for my band lesson at the end. The music teacher pulled me aside to tell me I needed to practice more—but I had been practicing *plenty* with my lip movements. He had not explained to me what notes were and how to produce them on this French horn monster. I was lost, and I felt like crying. What was I going to do?

That afternoon, I dutifully piled up my books; we had more homework than usual that night. I had gotten used to balancing the books in one arm (why didn't they have backpacks back then?) and my trusty French horn in the other. When the bell rang for dismissal at the end of the day, all the kids stepped out into the halls, single file, and headed for the buses. There was noise and laughter. I wasn't laughing. I was miserable. What was I going to tell my folks? They had rented the instrument for me and it wasn't cheap.

As I started down the hallway in the crowd of kids, I suddenly felt my underwear slide down a notch. In my haste earlier that morning, I had grabbed the only pair left in my bureau drawer. They were at the bottom of the drawer for a reason. Both of my hands were occupied, so I couldn't give them a hitch-up like I had been doing all day. I could feel my face turning crimson. Why had I put on those giant, stretched-out, waffle-textured undies? With each step, I could feel the undies slide down another inch. Why now? I thought in the mass confusion of exiting kids. Maybe if I took baby steps, it would slow the sliding process. If I could just get to the bus…

I slowed down and took one little baby step after another until a kid behind me said, "C'mon, hurry up! I wanna get home." So did I at this point. With every step my waffle-wear inched dangerously closer to my thighs. I was caught up in the flow of traffic, and there was no stopping. I reached desperately under my books to try and pull up the sagging undergarment, but I only succeeded in bunching up my skirt around my hips, leaving my leg exposed. I kept walking; the underwear kept doing the "slip-and-slide." I could see the buses ahead just outside the door. I was almost there. I spread my legs as wide as I could; if I could just stretch as wide as the elastic, I might hold them up. The effect was that of a waddling penguin. Then, like a slingshot, my underwear catapulted down my legs and plopped around my feet. I acted instinctively: I didn't look down; I didn't make eye contact with the kids around me; I stared straight ahead, head held high, French horn clutched in one hand, books in the other. With one deft shake of my foot, I stepped out of the underwear and kept walking.

As I walked home down the street that day, I felt like a load had been lifted from me. Maybe it was the release from an old pair of underwear, or maybe it was the release of knowing I would probably never play the French horn or have to carry it around again. My feet began to skip along the street as I danced to the sweet sounds of Tchaikovsky's *Peer Gynt Suite: Hall of the Mountain King* inside my head.

Can You Come Out to Play?

The day I got off the bus and announced that I had seen a house burned to the ground with a giant cross screaming *KKK* was the last straw for my parents. We were living in the South in the sixties, and we were surrounded by racial unrest and segregation. My parents were becoming increasingly alarmed at what was happening all around us. You couldn't go into the nearby city without seeing protests or rude signs with the cruel words "Whites Only" on them. My parents did not want me to grow up in a neighborhood of intolerance, mistrust, and cruelty toward people of color. There was much talk of moving in our house. While I understood firsthand why my parents were upset, I was upset for other reasons. I had made lots of friends in our three-block neighborhood. Having been an only child for ten years, I had hungered for company, and Dan Street was like heaven for me. With the talk of moving, I staged a few protests of my own, even threatening to run away. (The farthest I got was my best friend's house down the street.) My mom had roots in Maine, about as far north as you can get from Virginia, and Dad's family had summered on the Maine coast for years. It was familiar territory. When the final announcement came that we were going to move, our neighbors and friends could not understand why "y'all would move to Siberia." To them, we were migrating to the frozen tundra.

Dad quit his job, and Mom, a dutiful stay-at-home wife, packed us up. She would go wherever her husband went. My dad picked a seacoast town to live in and found a place listed under "Houses for Rent" in an *Uncle Henry's* magazine. The price of the rented house was just right for a family on the go. It took us two and a half days of hard travel to get there, my dad driving the U-Haul truck with an old Edsel hitched to the back. Mom drove our car, which was jam-packed with suitcases, a cooler of last-minute food from the refrigerator, and us kids. By this time, I was no longer an only child. I had a three-year-old sister and a newborn baby brother. I was in charge of the caretaking since Mom had all she could do to fight the heavy traffic and try to keep up with Dad.

We drove through the night on the second day and arrived in a sleepy town in Maine around three a.m. My dad pulled into the driveway of our landlord, knowing he would have to wake him up at this ungodly hour. Normally, I would have been mortified at this, but I was exhausted from riding in the car. Besides, my Italian fisherman's sweater had throw-up on it from burping my baby brother. I just wanted to lie down and go to sleep. Our house was around the corner from the landlord's. "Next to the stone library; you can't miss it," explained the landlord, who was none too impressed with our timing.

The house was a beautiful old two-story sea captain's house that looked exciting and promising from the outside. Dad and Mom unloaded a couple of mattresses and the baby crib, threw them on the living room floor, and we all crashed immediately. The next morning, we awoke to a freezing cold house. Were we really in Siberia? I wondered. Dad checked the basement furnace. It looked like there was oil in the tank near the furnace, but it didn't seem to be kicking in. We wrapped ourselves in blankets and surveyed our surroundings. We had no phone yet, so Dad went over to the landlord's once again to find out who could help us with the furnace.

There was a big kitchen with an old black cookstove nestled in one corner. The appliances looked worn from years of use. Mom checked the sink for running water, which, thankfully, was working. She started unpacking pans, bottles, and formula to feed my brother. My little sister toddled after me as I explored the rest of the house. It smelled old. The wooden floors were dark; the wallpaper on the walls was dark. Turning the corner from the living room, I gasped: There was a majestic walnut staircase that spiraled to the second floor. It was fit for royalty. Dragging our blankets behind us, my sister and I went up the stairs. If the staircase was majestic, the bedrooms were the opposite. The ceilings were high and rolled glass windows stretched from the floor to the ceiling. But the wallpaper was peeling everywhere. In fact, in one room, the ceiling was suspended in the middle of the room, ready to collapse with one strong wind or one swift toddler charging through the house. Now I knew why the price was right. This was a far cry from our modern tri-level house back on Dan Street.

I heard voices coming from downstairs. Male voices. One was my dad's. Had he found someone to fix the furnace? My sister and I hurried down the stairs and into the kitchen. A man with smiling, crinkly eyes, slightly balding, held out a rough red hand in greeting. "Mornin', miss," he said genially. We went through introductions.

"This is Floyd," Dad explained. "Apparently, he can fix anything," he continued.

"Don't know about that," Floyd said humbly. "Let's take a look at her." He motioned to the stairs of the basement, and the two went down to look things over.

We huddled around the oven, which my mom had turned on to throw off at least some heat, especially for my baby brother. Suddenly, we heard a loud *BOOM!* We jumped, then heard several booms in a row. A stream of expletives followed. "Son of a bitch! Goddamn it!" My mother and I looked at each other. It was definitely Floyd's voice. Was he talking to my dad like that? There was one more loud boom, and then we heard the hum of the furnace starting up. The washboards started to creak and groan.

Soon after, my dad and Floyd came up the stairs. Dad was smiling and shaking his head. Floyd nodded at him. "She just needed a little jump-start, is all," he said politely to my mom.

"Nothing like a few swift kicks," my dad added, motioning with his foot.

"Gotta go," Floyd said, pulling on an old baseball hat.

Dad pulled out his wallet. "How much do I—"

Beginnings

"No charge," Floyd said, waving him off and noticeably omitting the *r* in the word *charge*. "Welcome to our town."

• • •

Thus began our journey into small-town life. Even though we were "from away," the townspeople accepted us because we wanted to put our roots down there, and they responded with warmth and protectiveness. (It didn't hurt that my mom had grown up in Ellsworth...) Our neighborhood was brimming with kids, and I was able to make friends quickly, soon forgetting the hurt of leaving others behind. I finished high school there, went on to college, and returned a number of years later, where I met the new dentist in town while visiting my parents. I ended up marrying him! My husband's practice thrived in the tiny town. We decided to start a family and find a bigger house to live in rather than our cramped quarters over his office. It turned out that the house behind his office on the next street was in foreclosure. It needed a ton of work, but Loren loved projects. We took the plunge and bought the house.

Our new yellow house was one of many houses on the quiet street just off the main drag in town. Our neighborhood was steeped in classic New England architecture. Across the street stood the Congregational Church. Its white steeple stood high above the trees, reminding everyone which direction heaven was in. On either side of the church were museum buildings. These were once private homes that had been taken over and remodeled by benefactors who wanted to perpetuate the history of the sea captains and their impact on the town. Lining the rest of the street were clapboard and shingled houses, small and cozy, suggesting an intimacy and protectiveness in the neighborhood. The houses were bursting with kids. This was the quintessential neighborhood in my mind: a slow traffic street, lots of friendly people, institutions of faith and stability, and a playground haven for my kids. It was soon apparent that the kids in the neighborhood were as diverse and intriguing as the characters in a Norman Rockwell painting. They each made themselves known to my family in a most unique way.

Can You Come Out to Play?

The Twins

The twins, Andy and Blake, were adorable. They were a year older than my son. They lived behind our yellow house on the adjacent street. They were rough-and-tumble kids, and my son couldn't wait to mix it up with them. No one could tell the twins apart except their family, but I always thought one of them had a narrower, more angular face than the other. Andy was tenderhearted: He loved animals and had a way with them. He could also knock his twin brother over with a swift kick to the shins or stomach. Blake was the more serious of the two: He was the analytical one. That manifested in daily war play. He knew the strategies of where to hide so that he could bombard his brother and my son with rotten apples that he found on the grass in our yard. The three boys wrestled, played, and climbed wildly on the swing set in our backyard. My son was the happiest when the two boys would come to the back door and ask, "Can Ben come out to play?" That could be as early as 7 a.m. or after dinner before dark set in.

One day when I was working in the kitchen, the three boys opened the back door. Andy was carrying something in his hand. It was wriggling, and the boys were grinning from ear to ear. "Look what we found," Andy said proudly. He held out the two-foot-long, wriggling garter snake for me to take. I nearly passed out.

"Wow," I said, "that's amazing, but I think he would be happier back in the garden. Take him right outside, OK?" I backed away toward the sink, a frozen smile on my face.

The three boys laughed, turned, and ran out the door. I grabbed the sink and watched them out the window as they passed the poor critter back and forth between them. Utterly fearless. The three of them always seemed to find something fun to do, although it worried me when they used plastic or cardboard swords to swat at each other. There were plenty of admonishments to put these poke-your-eye-out weapons away, but somehow, they always resurfaced.

In the fall of that year, the twins announced they were going to move. It was only a mile up the road, but to my son, it was a million miles away. No longer would they be able to meet every day in the field beside our house, play hide-and-seek, or host apple war games.

The day before they moved, the three boys climbed into my husband's parked runabout boat in the driveway. Together, they raised their cardboard swords high in the air with a war cry. Their love and loyalty to each other was unmistakable. The "Three Musketeers" would be forever bound to one another.

The next day, Ben got up early. He climbed up on the couch in the kitchen that looked out a window to the backyard where the move behind our house was already in progress. He didn't budge from his perch all morning, nor did he want any breakfast. It was the saddest thing I had ever seen. His heart was broken and so was mine.

In spite of the move, the three boys found their way back to each other through middle school, high school, and beyond. Trouble, though not malicious, was never far behind when the three reunited.

■ *Both twins went into the armed services after high school; Ben went on to college. The three boys parted ways for a time, but always seemed to reconnect throughout the years. In spite of severe emotional scars from active military duty, the twins remain true to their loyal friend, my son, the third Musketeer.*

Rosey

"Rosey," as we called her, ran the neighborhood on our seemingly quiet little street. She was only five years old but had already seen a lot of real life right in her own backyard. The true identity of her father was never determined, although my best friend, who lived next door to the lively household, reported that a very strange guy sometimes showed up at all times of the day or night. At one point, he set fire to some tires in the yard, which caused quite a stir. Police cars and a fire engine showed up when a worried neighbor called it in. Police cars were regular guests at Rosey's house. Domestic disputes were frequent. Rosey's mom, a child herself, and her mother, a very obese woman with thick glasses, stringy hair, and a foul mouth, had frequent shouting matches with the male stranger who showed up unannounced. It wasn't long after one of these rounds that Rosey's mom became pregnant. All these circumstances made Rosey a very independent little scrapper. She was basically on her own and didn't seem to mind it one bit. She looked angelic—long, stick-straight dark hair with ramrod-straight Dutch-girl bangs and almond-shaped blue eyes that could snap and crackle if someone rubbed her the wrong way. She had a round face and a mischievous grin; you couldn't help but like her, even though you wanted to be sure nothing was missing after she visited your house. Rosey frequently showed up at our front door wanting to come in and see our daughter. She roamed the neighborhood at will, organizing kids to come out and play. She had a raspy, grating voice and was very loud—a defense mechanism from her life at home. We liked Rosey but always had her wait on the porch until my daughter was ready to go out. This stemmed from the time that Rosey made her way into a neighbor's house and helped herself to a giant piece of pie that was on the kitchen counter. No one got mad at her, and no one on the street locked their doors at night despite her escapades. Everyone understood why she acted as she did.

■ *Rosey managed to finish high school in the town, but followed the only path she had ever known, becoming pregnant barely out of high school, just a child herself. Her family eventually moved from the neighborhood, and everyone breathed a sigh of relief. People still smile, though, at the mention of her name.*

Katy and Jessie

My daughter, Katy, and her friend, Jessie, who lived down the street, were inseparable chums. They clicked immediately after we moved to the neighborhood. Jessie was the younger of the two by about a year and a half. She was the sweetest little girl ever—to everyone but boys. In this case, the boys were her brother, Justin, and Katy's brother, Ben. It was immediately apparent that no one was going to boss her around. Both boys were older and had tried to apply their natural pecking order to no avail. Justin quickly learned to back off and stay out of his sister's path; Ben, on the other hand, was very stubborn and bossy and met Jessie head-on. The two clashed whenever they were in the same room.

Katy, who was also an independent little girl at the time, loved Jessie's spirit. The two girls would meet in the field near our houses, carrying notepads and pencils with them. This was the beginning of their espionage adventures. Their goal was to spy on and record the activities of the adults and kids of the neighborhood. They frequently hid behind trees and houses to sit and write their findings. In the summer, these espionage events would continue well after dark. The girls would reluctantly return home after repeated summonses to come in for the night. On one such night, the girls had hidden behind the big white church near our house. When I called to my daughter to come in, she and Jessie ran into the house bursting with excitement.

"Mom, Mom, you'll never guess who we just saw through the window of the church! It was one of the guys that works at school! He was at a meeting!" This stopped me in my tracks. "What kind of meeting was that, anyway?" my daughter asked.

"That's the weekly AA meeting, Katy."

Katy and Jessie were old enough to realize what their findings meant. The two of them looked at each other, mouths open in shock. That was a teachable moment for me with the two girls. It was also the end of the Espionage Ring.

■ *Katy went off to college in a state far away from her hometown and the street of her childhood. Jessie stayed home and tried nursing school but found she didn't really like it. The two girls have kept in touch over the years. When Katy met the man of her dreams, she came home to ask Jessie to be in her wedding party. When Jessie, Katy, Jessie's mom, Julie, and I all went out to dinner to celebrate the event, Katy proposed a toast. Jessie thought it was a toast to the bride. In fact, it was a toast to Jessie. "Jessie, will you be my maid of honor?" Katy asked, as she turned toward her spy cohort, her dear friend of many years. The shock on Jessie's face was obvious. She knew Katy had moved away and made many new friends from college and grad school. The distance between them was thousands of miles. But not the distance of their friendship. "Of course," Jessie replied, as we all clinked glasses, eyes and hearts filled to the brim.*

Larry

While our street was a tight-knit little community, once in a while there was an infiltrator. In this case, it was Larry. No one knew where Larry lived or exactly how old he was (we all guessed about eight or nine), but everyone knew him by sight. He was always riding around town on his rickety red bicycle. He loved this bike even though he lacked the coordination to even ride it—it was almost too big for him to manage. The result was wobbly, and the bike looked like it would topple over any minute. Sometimes you would see the bike in a heap by the local grocer's; other times it lay precariously balanced against the side of someone's house.

Larry's lack of coordination might have been related to his vision. He wore extra-thick glasses that were too big for his face and were held together with Scotch tape. Steering the bike and pushing the glasses up on his nose at the same time was too much for him, but he managed to keep going. When he rode down the street, the kids would wave to him, but they didn't quite trust him. He seemed to appear out of nowhere at odd times and then disappear just as quickly. One Saturday morning, my husband answered a knock on our front door. Larry stood at the door, smiling the biggest buck-toothed smile he could muster. He brushed his shaggy hair out of his eyes and announced, "Bottle Drive!"

"Really?" Loren said, amused. "And who's this bottle drive for?"

"Me!" Larry said boldly.

I think my husband scraped up a few bottles to help Larry's cause. How could you say no to that bold a request?

■ *We don't know what happened to Larry. He eventually stopped riding his bicycle around town, and somewhere today, he's probably a fundraiser for some worthy institution.*

George

If ever there was a candidate for a Norman Rockwell painting, George was it. Tall and extremely skinny at the tender age of eleven, freckle-faced, wide-eyed, tow-headed George was a smiley kid. Goofy and friendly to all, George was accepted easily into the neighborhood network. He and his older sister, Henrietta, were renters across the street from our house. They had a mother that you never saw and a guy living with her. "That's my mom's boyfriend," George would explain. The boyfriend smoked cigarettes frantically and yelled at

George and Henrietta whenever he stepped outside. They stayed out of his way. The two kids constantly roamed the neighborhood looking for something to do.

One day my son, Ben, and the twins were playing a game of pick-up baseball in our yard when George came over to join them. He was allowed to be up immediately as the new guest player. Tall and lanky, George quickly discovered that he could hit the ball. He sent the boys running after several long hits. He had one more swing before giving up his turn to my son. Ben stood behind him, taking on the role of catcher. George swung the bat, ready to make contact with the ball one of the Twins pitched to him. Unfortunately, the only contact made was with Ben's eye. He was standing too close behind George. The bat caught him squarely above his eye and under his eyebrow. There was a bloodcurdling scream that echoed down the street. All action stopped as my son came running into the house, holding his eye.

My sister was visiting me at the time, and my husband was away in Minnesota. Jen and I had been chatting it up when Ben burst into the room screaming, "My eyeball fell out, my eyeball fell out!" Blood was everywhere. All over Ben's face, his shirt, his hands as he clutched his eye. These were not exactly the words a mother or an aunt or even the neighborhood kids wanted to hear. My sister called the hospital to tell them we were coming. My heart sank. Oh, my God! His eyeball! I grabbed some towels and pressed them against Ben's face. He refused to remove his hand. As we made a dash for the car, George and the twins looked on in shock. "I'm so sorry, I'm so sorry," George muttered over and over. He and the twins looked like they were going to cry. How could they play baseball with Ben if he had only one eye?

As it turned out, Ben's eyeball did not fall out. It only *felt* that way because the flap of skin under the brow had given way. He needed three stitches to make him feel whole again. When we returned, the boys were waiting in the yard. George apologized then to Ben, who mumbled, "That's OK." Everyone was sent home so I could recover from the ordeal. Ben lay in front of the TV with ice on his face. I used the ice in glasses of wine for my sister and myself. We all recovered nicely.

George came to check on Ben for the next several days. In fact, the whole neighborhood of kids stopped by to see his war wounds. Shortly after that, George and his sister moved on. There was a domestic disturbance one night and the police showed up. Apparently, the "boyfriend" was threatening George's mother with a gun. In contrast to this, Ben's stitches seemed minimal. We all missed George's sweet demeanor, but we were happy to see them go.

■ *We finally moved from the yellow house to our new house on the lake an hour away from so many memories. Not long ago, I visited my dear friend Julie, who still lives on the same street where our kids grew up. "We got a new batch of kids on the block now," she told me. "I think there's a story in there somewhere."*

Family Ties

Katy-Did

My daughter, Katy, literally skidded into the world with full intent.

I nearly gave birth to her on the way to the hospital. I was totally unprepared for how quickly the labor process moved along. After all, my previous child had been born after twenty-two hours of hard labor, complete with Pitocin to induce contractions, followed by two hours of hard pushing. My son, a beautiful boy, had arrived—stubborn and defiant—on his own good time.

It was easy to assume that I had much hard work ahead of me that March night when my contractions started. But boy, was I wrong. By the time I reached the hospital, I could barely walk. Contractions were coming quickly, just a few minutes apart. The nurses wheeled me in and set me up in a birthing room. They exchanged worried glances. I noticed. I concentrated on my breathing to ease the contractions, which weren't overwhelming but seemed pretty continuous. At one point, I heard one of the nurses say, "We can do it." The older nurse looked down at me then, smiled sweetly, and said, "The doctor is on his way. Cross your legs and breathe deeply."

I must have been in transition just then because the younger nurse, who bent down to adjust the baby heart monitor, was within reach of my hand. My hand shot out and caught the collar of her crisp uniform. With the strength of a hundred elephants, I pulled her by the collar so that her face was smushed up against my cheek. The look of surprise on her face matched my own, but I was desperate. "*I'm having this baby now*," I hissed in an alien voice. She nodded, still shocked by my deft maneuver, and stood back, looking askance to the older, wiser nurse.

I sat up, sweating profusely, ready to move mountains, but all I really wanted to do was expel this baby. The urge to push was overwhelming. My husband, who was in the room, said simply, "I think it's time."

Just then the doctor walked in. I remember a fleeting thought that he didn't look awake yet (it was, after all, three a.m.). Could he deliver my baby when he was half asleep? I looked at him and said, "Now?"

He replied, Now," and within seconds, Katy slid out like a force of nature.

Once the nurses cleaned her up, she was beautiful, just like my son, Ben, had been. I did notice two little red lines on her forehead and questioned the younger nurse about these. The nurse smiled warily at me (how else could she act after engaging with a Sumo wrestler?) and told me that they called those lines "stork bites." It happened sometimes during the birthing process, she explained, but they would disappear within a day or so. To me, they looked like skid marks, and Katy had, indeed skidded into the world in less than four hours.

My little "force of nature" stayed true to her designation. She was fearless and did everything in a forthright, unaffected manner. One day I needed to return some merchandise to a store in the next town over. I had Katy, who was a toddler at the time, and Ben, who was about four, with me. The store was very busy. I kept a tight hold on Katy's hand. Ben was instructed to hold tightly to her other hand, which he did, happy to be in charge. I stepped up to the Returns desk and laid my package on the counter. The clerk smiled at me and the two adorable children I had with me. I let go of Katy's hand for a moment to complete my transaction. Within seconds, I heard snickers all around me, then heard Ben say, "Katy, stop it." I looked down beside me into Katy's smiling face—and she was stark naked. She had disrobed in about sixty seconds. Her clothes lay in a crumpled heap at her feet. She was deliriously happy, unencumbered and free. The clerk broke out in laughter and so did everyone in the store as I quickly dressed her in spite of her protests.

Taking my little nudist to the grocery store was less risky because she had to sit in the cart. Fortunately, her surroundings distracted her. She was fascinated with everything. Her luminous eyes and smile lit up her face and the faces of everyone else who saw her. She was adorable with her dimples and laughter. Little old ladies cooed and clucked when they saw her. All was well until I noticed on one particular occasion that one of these sweet little old ladies came up to her in the cart for a closer interaction. Who wouldn't want to touch that lovely little button nose? As I turned with a carton of milk in my hand, I noticed a change come over Katy's face. Her smile disappeared; her eyes narrowed. She had turned into a demon child in split seconds. The little old lady, startled by this sudden change, backed away in fear and toddled over to her friend to describe what had happened. I was amazed, too, but as I looked at Katy again, her smile had returned. Who was this child, anyway?

It was quickly apparent that Katy was far from possessed. She would wake up in the morning smiling or singing as she lay in her bed. Her dad and I were astonished, mostly because I was the antithesis of this in the mornings. I needed at least two cups of coffee before my smile appeared, and singing? Well, that happened after a glass or two of wine on the weekends. Loren, so touched by his daughter's sweetness, frequently went in before he left for work and wiggled her little toe as she lay sleeping. Her response was a smile, eyes closed or not. Then she would pop out of bed, hug her daddy, and pull on her clothes for the day. Or rather, I should say, *the same clothes* for the day. Ever the force of nature, Katy knew what she wanted to wear, and that was simple: her Rainbow Brite shirt. It had a little girl on it next to a pony with a magically colored mane. Katy had a collection of all the toys from this line, and she loved them all. She wore the shirt every day. The only time I could get it off her was when she put on her pajamas at night. Then I would sneak the shirt into the laundry, ready for the next day's adventures.

Katy's love of her Rainbow Brite shirt was not her only obsession. She was not happy with her hair. She couldn't understand why her mommy, daddy, and even her older brother had thick heads of hair: Why didn't *she*? One night, as we watched TV in the family room, Katy got up to go to the bathroom. When she didn't return after a few minutes, I went to check on her. I opened the bathroom door to find her sitting next to the sink, a giant pair of scissors in her hand (what kind of Mother *was* I???) and the biggest, most satisfied smile on her face. Hair was everywhere. I screamed from the shock, and as soon as I did, so did she. We both started crying—me from the fact that my daughter looked like a war victim, with little tufts of hair all over her head and no bangs visible, and she from disappointment that her new look was not appreciated.

After that, the family phrase became "look what Katy did." We got through it, but all I could think of was that someone would report me for not watching my kids; in fact, a few weeks earlier, my son had experienced lice—actually just he and I experienced it (a great moment for me). My husband had been so paranoid he'd shaved Ben's head. Unfortunately, the shaver was dull, and there were unsightly clumps of hair left on his head, and he appeared monkey-like because his ears were now quite visible. The glasses the poor kid had to wear didn't help the overall effect either... That same week, I saw Ben's teacher, whom I knew pretty well. "What happened to your kids?" she asked me, barely stifling a giggle. "They look like war victims!" *I* was just worried that someone was going to report me to Child Protection Services.

Katy, my little force of nature, adapted to her new look. She simply added an "extension" to her hair: an old piece of long lace material she found in my closet. She wore it on her head proudly everywhere she went, tossing the long "locks" back over her shoulders. She reminded me of a nursery-school bride who made a stunning fashion statement in her Rainbow Brite shirt.

Katy and Ben, who squabbled like most siblings, could at least agree on one thing: They truly loved my husband's parents. Unfortunately, they lived in Minnesota, almost 2,000 miles from our home in Maine. When we did visit them, the kids were entertained from morning till night. There were rides on the tractor with Grandpa (I nearly fainted when I looked out the window and my son, who was about five at the time, was driving the tractor...), there was always something yummy cooking with Grandma, and new toys to be opened. The kids loved every minute we spent with them.

It was a shock to us all when Grandma died, though she had been valiantly battling cancer for a number of years. We had to make the long trek back to Minnesota for the funeral. Growing up in my parents' house, there was little talk of funerals. If someone died, it was quickly glossed over with my brother, my sister, and I, and we were not allowed to go to funerals. Looking back, I think my parents thought it was a way to protect us, but the truth was, it made it even harder to deal with the natural passages in life. I was therefore the skittish one when we flew out to Minnesota for Grandma's funeral. I had been to exactly one funeral in my life, and that was my dad's. I had little or no coping mechanisms to deal with this and had spent a good year in therapy trying to understand the grief process. I didn't want my own kids to be so sheltered that they would not be able to get through a catastrophe like this. Loren and I had talked frankly with them about what to expect at the funeral home and at the church service. They took it in stride. Katy was about three at the time and was more upset about seeing her daddy cry than about what we were going to experience. I, on the other hand, had quivering nerves in my belly.

When we arrived at the funeral home two days later, I hung back from the crowd that had come to pay their respects to Katy's Grandma. My husband and his sister took charge of the situation. As people entered, they hugged Loren and his sister and walked up to the casket where Grandma lay in repose. I was clutching Katy's hand, and my son stood right next to me, leaning against me. All of a sudden, Katy let go of my hand. I thought she was walking toward her dad, so I let her go, watching her carefully. Like the force of nature that she was, Katy walked right by her dad and marched up to the casket. "Katy—" I called out, not knowing what she would do and terrified that she might freak out at the sight of her still grandma. The crowd parted then to watch the little girl peek over the edge of her grandmother's casket.

I ran up behind her, but Loren motioned for me to stay back. We watched. Katy didn't utter a word. Instead she reached into the casket. Grandma was holding a handkerchief and wearing a pretty flowered dress. Around her neck was a string of pearls. Ever so gently, Katy rearranged the handkerchief and then the pearls. I let out a muffled sob. But I wasn't the only one. The entire room started to weep. I knew in that moment that Katy's simple gesture had released their emotions, so they could grieve in a natural way. I learned something that day from my bold, fearless daughter. Look what Katy did, I thought.

• • •

By first and second grade, Katy's focus had turned toward dolls, namely Barbie and Ken. She now had a thick head of hair that matched the long, luxurious locks of her Barbies. She had turned her bedroom into a Barbieville Community. Everyone had given her a new Barbie for every occasion. She had also collected a Barbie camper, a deluxe red car, a Barbie house, and even a Barbie bus. I frequently heard Barbie dialogue as I went by her room or Barbie singing, (one of the Barbies was a nightclub singer). The introduction of Ken to the bevy of Barbies created quite a stir in Barbieville: I began to notice that all the Barbies were naked, including Ken. I had flashbacks to my toddler disrobing and wondered if this was a Freudian moment for my daughter, but I dismissed the thought. Years later, Katy joked that she had, indeed, been fascinated with Ken's "nub," as she called it. We reminisced about the day I had come in to clean her room. There were decapitated Barbies with heads scattered around the floor. The rest of the naked Barbies were piled up in a heap with Ken proudly on top. But that wasn't all: Katy's Barbie horse topped the whole pile. When questioned, Katy explained that the pile was the work of her brother, Ben. He loved to tease and torture his little sister. Had I been worrying about the wrong child?

In spite of my worries, Katy and Ben continued their childhoods in a somewhat normal pattern. Katy's days of playing with her Barbies passed, and by fourth grade, she believed she was a Whitney Houston incarnate. She knew every song that Whitney sang by heart, and she wanted the world to hear her sing. The world, at that time, turned out to be her family and the family of her best friend, Jessie, down the street. We were privy to special concerts on Saturday nights in our kitchen. Katy would don a black curly wig (there's that hair thing again…), grab her pretend microphone, and belt out Whitney's latest hit. Jessie sang backup with Katy for some of the songs. Jessie's dad videotaped the shows, creating precious memories for us all. Katy's love of singing followed her through middle and high school. She sang and acted in plays and later auditioned for an a cappella group at her college.

■ *Today Katy works on a team in a large corporation. Her focus has changed from singing, nudity, and special-edition haircuts to communications. She can still light up a room with her smile and gorgeous, long blond hair, but don't be deceived by her sweetness: She is a force of nature to be reckoned with when fierce conversations are needed. As this is written, she is due to have her first child—a girl—sometime after the Christmas holidays. And somewhere in the back of my clothes drawer is a tiny Rainbow Brite shirt just waiting to find its new, bold owner.*

Boat Launch

The *Linnea* rested quietly in its special nook in the garage for twenty years.

Twenty years before, it had been hauled 2,000 miles from Minnesota to Maine after the death of my father-in-law. It was a poignant reminder that its former captain wasn't there to take the tiller anymore. My husband had a garage built next to his office to house this twenty-eight-foot sailboat. He saw the boat every time he went to the garage from his office. This was a daily occurrence because he had also carved a small apartment out of one corner of the garage's second floor and used this space to eat his lunch in during the workday.

The garage also served another purpose: It provided storage space for every box of his parents' belongings that had been shipped along with the boat. Every space in the garage was utilized—the walls, the cupboards, the closets. Even the tiny attic that capped this mausoleum contained tools, boxes, dishes, lamps, and pictures from a lifetime of memories. Loren was too heartbroken to open any boxes with the exception of his father's tools. Those he unpacked and spread out along a tool bench on one side of the garage or hung them on the wall with a promise to use them. But the *Linnea* remained a silent giant in a dark bay of the garage; it was just too big a reminder of days and people of the past.

In spite of the sadness we felt, we carried on with our lives. We had two wonderful children who kept us busy through elementary, middle, and high school. Ben, the oldest, went away to a college in Pennsylvania. It was more difficult to drop him off at college than we had anticipated—so much so that my husband drove down a one-way street going the wrong way right after we dropped him off, while I sat and sobbed in the car. Loren had convinced Ben that this college was a great one, and that he would get a great education. We survived the separation but missed our son greatly. At Christmastime when he came home, he came to see me one day at the school where I taught. Everyone had left for the day. Ben settled himself in a student's desk and began to talk. He was generally a quiet person, similar to his dad, but when he had something to say, he was forthright. He spoke about missing his friends here in Maine and how far away the college was, and that he really didn't like it anyway. I listened, but I didn't really hear the intensity behind his words. I reassured him that it was natural to feel homesick and that there were many ways to stay in touch with his friends. After the holiday, he dutifully returned to college.

About a month later, a catastrophic event occurred: Ben was caught with pot in his dorm room. He had to withdraw from the school. We were shocked, devastated, angry, scared, and grieving for our son's calamity, and he came home with very similar feelings. He was angry at us, the college, the police, the world; he felt no one was listening to him. At the time, we were living in the tiny apartment in the garage with our daughter, who was a sophomore in high school. We had bought land near a lake in a town about an hour north and were in the process of building a house. The apartment was already cramped, but now Ben would be staying here, too. Loren told him that he could live with us if he got a job, but first things first. He took Ben downstairs to the workshop area, past the silent *Linnea*, to the area where all his dad's tools were—and told him that he needed to build a bed for himself.

With Loren's help, the task got started the very night Ben came home. The hum of Grandpa's saw echoed loudly through the garage over the next several nights. Ben got a landscaping job in a nearby town, and hearts started to heal. By fall, we had all moved into our beautiful home on the lake, and Ben decided to go back to college—but this time, he enrolled at a local university—and went on to become a mechanical engineer. We were immensely proud of him.

When the time came for him to move out of the house and start a new job and a life on his own, we were overjoyed at his success. Loren and I wept openly as soon as he drove out of the dooryard. Katy went away to college in the South, and we became the classic definition of "empty-nesters." We got used to being without our kids and eventually created a new life for ourselves. We were fortunate that Ben lived only about three hours away from us, but we were not as lucky with our daughter—she had moved to Arkansas, three plane rides away from us. We usually saw her at least twice a year—not nearly enough—but we went on with our lives and our careers, and before we knew it, we were face to face with retirement.

My husband still owned the office and the garage in the small town south of us: Wouldn't that be a logical place to retire to, at least temporarily? We could live in the apartment over the garage and save a bundle of money. That way, we could travel, visit our kids, and maybe find a small cottage somewhere in the South during the winter months. We would have gone "full circle"—back to the town where I had grown up, back to the place where Loren had started his business, but also back to the garage where the *Linnea* was still a silent reminder of family.

We were at the garage one weekend contemplating what to do with all those boxes we had stored there when Loren, whose knees had begun to plague him, announced that he was going to sell his dad's boat. It was difficult for him to get around on land, much less maneuver around a sailboat, which, due to years of dormancy, would need major maintenance. I was stunned by this announcement because I knew the sentimental feelings my husband had for the boat. I understood, though, as I could plainly see that he would be facing knee replacement in the very near future. We told our kids about our retirement plans and about selling the boat. They, too, were surprised, even though all of us had ignored the silent giant in the garage for years.

About a month or so after this announcement, Ben had an announcement of his own. He was going to quit his job of ten years and travel with his girlfriend to Nepal and Thailand for three months.

We were excited for him, but also a little nervous—would he have enough money to live on to do all of this? Would he get a job again when he returned? He reassured us he had quite a nest egg and would be just fine. "Go and live your life, then," we told him. His plan was to leave in late September. He had the summer to reclaim a less stressful and relatively worry-free life and to prepare for his trip. Several weeks after his announcement, he came to visit us. He talked excitedly about his trip: a hike on the Anna Purna Circuit with a guide and off to the jungles of Thailand after that. What an opportunity!

"There's something else I want to do, Dad," he added. "Let's get the boat in the water this summer."

Nothing could have shocked us more. We could not believe our ears. Ben had never really shown an interest in the boat—nor any other project with his dad except that distant time when he and his dad had literally built a bed for him to lie in. That had been a painful time for all of us. Now here he was, resurrecting—no, *saving*—the *Linnea* from an unknown destiny.

Shortly after this, despite Loren's bad knees, amazing things started to happen: There were decks to scrub, temperature sensors to install, bilges to pump out, motors to turn over, sails to mend. The *Linnea* stood majestically outside of the garage in all her glory, her mast straight and taut, waiting for her two capable captains to take her tiller in hand. One day as Loren and Ben were working together and deep in conversation about how to rewire a section of the sailboat, I noticed a beautiful red cardinal sitting on a branch in a nearby tree. I had not seen this bird in our area before and I was struck by its beautiful color. I had a sudden flashback to a time in Minnesota when we had visited my husband's family and had gone for a sail on the *Linnea*. Grandpa's yard had been full of cardinals—he loved them and had bird feeders everywhere. As I looked at the cardinal again, there was no doubt in my mind that everyone's heart was smiling on this day—young and old, past and present.

Can You Dig It?

Several years ago, I took a class at a nearby university. It was a class of only seven people, so we got to know each other pretty quickly. As the class unfolded, I was dumbfounded at the connections I had with at least five of the seven participants. One of them lived in a nearby town called Surry. That piqued my interest immediately. My dad's family had owned property in Surry years before, and his family had come to Maine for the summers. Dad and his brother had built a log cabin one summer on part of the property. I mentioned this to the woman from Surry, and she remarked, "Oh, yeah, I live two houses down the road from that cabin."

But this wasn't the only connection in that class. One day as we were talking, it came out that I had grown up in the town of Searsport. A young girl taking the class piped up, "Searsport? My mom graduated from high school there." As it turned out, her mother knew me because I was an upperclassman at the time. I recognized her picture, but she had been a sophomore when I was a senior. There was a ripple effect that day. Another older woman chimed in, "You lived in Searsport? I was a principal at the Stockton Elementary School." This school was about six miles from Searsport—and I had taught at that school for fifteen years. She had become principal the year I left. We had lots to chat about.

Then there was the wife of a guy who was currently teaching with me. I had never met her in the eight years I had taught at the nearby big-city school. Unbelievable! The last class member I connected with was a visiting poet who had joined our class for part of the semester. He kept staring at me. I finally asked him if I knew him from somewhere. He said, "I gotta tell you, I can't stop staring at you because you are a dead ringer for my best friend in Vermont. You look just like her." He said she was a professor at a college in Vermont, so I looked her up online. She *did* kind of look like me. It was possible we were connected. My dad had been a busy guy in Vermont as a traveling salesman. To this day, my siblings and I wonder if we might have some half-brothers or -sisters floating around out there…

All of these connections just blew my mind, but don't we all have stories of coincidences like these?

Last year, I was grocery shopping one day when I noticed a woman I had never seen before rounding the fresh vegetable aisle. Our eyes met, and we smiled at each other. We kept bumping into each other throughout the store. We were laughing by the fourth time we ran into each other, but we never spoke. The next day, the home health care nurse, who was coming to tend to Loren with his knee replacement, knocked on my door. Yep, you guessed it. It was the same lady I had seen in the store! We both gasped and laughed and talked about this uncanny coincidence. But was it a coincidence? Was it fate? What the heck was going on?

Was the Universe trying to tell me something? I really wasn't convinced that the Fates might be playing a role rather than coincidence until an incident happened while I was teaching at a big-city middle school.

I had been teaching at this school for about fourteen years. I absolutely loved teaching, and I was always looking for new and exciting ways to reach my students. We were about to start a unit on ancient Greece when I had a moment of inspiration. Why not connect the ruins of Greece to the unused courtyard that sat idly in the middle of our school? We could create an archaeology dig: I would bury Greek artifacts that I made or borrowed in a gridded area in a corner of the courtyard. My students could learn how an archaeologist uses coordinates to unearth one grid section at a time—then the research on their discoveries could begin. I was so excited by this idea that I began an immediate search on the web for a real-life archaeologist in the vicinity of our school who might be willing to help us out. I tried the nearby university, but the professors were either too busy or were away on a dig. Undaunted, I knew I could still conduct a dig of my own. I wanted to share my idea and get permission to use the courtyard from the principal, but when I went to his office, I learned he was out of the building. His secretary, whom I knew well, was all ears about my new project. "Oh, I know some archaeologists," she offered.

"What? You do? Who?"

"They are a husband and wife who live in Stockton Springs, right where you taught for years. You know, out on the Cape. I know them because my daughters go to gymnastics class with their daughters. They're really nice people. I bet they'd help you out if you asked them."

I couldn't believe my luck! The secretary lived just minutes from the tiny town of Stockton Springs where I had been an elementary teacher for many years. This news of the archaeologists was perfect. I was on a mission. A few weeks later, I headed down the coast toward Stockton. I had tried to contact the archaeologists but to no avail. But that did not deter me. I didn't want to arrive at their house unannounced, but I was curious about them because I knew the area well. On the way through Stockton, I stopped at the Trenton General Store. Sure enough, the clerk recognized me from high school and was more than happy to help. She knew where the archaeologists lived and scribbled down the address. It wasn't familiar because, as the clerk explained it, the mailboxes had all been renumbered with the influx of retired people and new condos out on the Cape. As I rounded the Cape Road—Cape Jellison, it was called—I took in the beautiful surroundings. The Cape was a mix of majestic sea captain's houses, dilapidated trailers, and modern condos—a mix that didn't sit well with the original "townies." But, oh, the water views! I had a pang of nostalgia. I had loved this little town and its school and all its students. I started checking mailbox numbers—1205, 1206, 1207, 1208—that was it! 1208! I signaled to the right and pulled off just ahead of the mailbox. I looked to the left at the house across the road and suddenly realized where I was. I was overcome with emotion. My eyes filled, my throat bubbled, my heart pounded.

It was none other than my own grandmother's house. The archaeologists were living in my grandmother's old house.

I could picture her standing there. Her snow-white hair cut in a bob, her thick glasses sitting atop her strong nose, her shirttail flapping as the sea breeze kicked up, and her short-shorts showing off her beautiful legs. She had always been proud of those legs. Everyone called her "Bine," but no one knew where that bizarre name had come from. She laughed when my siblings and I asked her about it and told us her husband had given her that nickname. Her real name was Irene, but even her six brothers and sisters never called her that growing up. (There was a family secret floating around that suggested this was the same name as a mistress her father had. Was she the result of that tryst? No one knew...) As I stood in shock at the edge of the road, I recalled images of Bine's homemade cookies, which she always kept in her fridge, along with the cheap large bottles of wine that she drank generously. (I didn't tell my mom for years that she always let us kids have some wine when we spent the night with her. We thought we were very grown-up but looking back, I think she just wanted us to go to bed early.) Bine was fun and quirky, and I loved her deeply. She read books voraciously and dabbled in paintings of fields and flowers and little children running in them. She sang lullabies to me when I was little: "*Hush, hush, hush, here comes the Dream Man*" was one of her favorites. I could hear her deep, alto voice: "*Now little Patsy, run up the stairs. Put on your nightie and say your prayers.*" She could also belt out the best of any Irish lyrics at a moment's notice. She labeled every item in her house with the name of the person it would go to after her death. This always freaked me and my siblings out. "Don't drop that vase. It's meant for your Aunt Gloria," would make us pause and quickly return it to the shelf. Bine was eccentric, and a rebel, and I know that's why I identified with her.

And here I stood in front of her house—no, the archaeologists' house now—tears streaming down my face. Suddenly, a dog barked wildly, and I saw two little girls scoot to the back of the house. Apparently, they had seen the strange woman crying across the street and gone inside for safety. I realized how I must have appeared and tried to wipe the mascara away from my eyes as a man and a woman came out of the house and peered at me.

"Oh, hello!" I called out. I quickly explained who I was and what I was doing there (and mentioning the school secretary helped!). I could see them visibly relax. "I was overcome when I realized you lived in my grandmother's house," I told them. We spoke for quite a while about my school idea, and then they revealed that they had discovered a Native American burial site underneath the house. My grandmother had always complained that she felt a presence in the house, and she sometimes heard loud noises at night and couldn't sleep because of them. The archaeologists had discovered pieces of arrowheads while digging up the garden the previous spring, and this had led them to explore further.

They agreed to come to my school forty-five minutes away and help out with the dig, and as I drove away, I was consumed with thoughts of my grandmother. Was it a coincidence that I had decided to do an archaeology dig and that the archaeologists were living in my grandmother's house? Or was Fate stepping in, reminding me of what was important and what or who should be cherished and not forgotten? On my way home, I stopped at the Trenton General Store and called Loren to tell him what had happened.

Unfortunately, the archaeologists never came to my school for the dig because one of their daughters came down with pneumonia. They did loan me all the equipment, however, which I picked up from them before the dig. As I watched my class of middle schoolers "discovering" the Greek artifacts in each square of our gridded courtyard, I smiled to myself. Perhaps one day, Fate would guide them to rediscover a long-lost but never forgotten memory.

Up at the Cabin

There is a tiny, stucco cabin sitting on a knoll by Borden Lake in Garrison, Minnesota. The cabin is steeped in tradition and is the keeper of family stories, specifically the family stories of the Swedes—the Bergs and the Carlsons. Gust Berg, a plasterer by trade, crafted the tiny but sturdy cabin back in the 1930s. The kitchen, with its vintage Frigidaire and old gas stove, anachronisms by today's standards, remains steadfast, these ancient appliances rooted in their exact same spots. All the fresh hopes of Gust and Astrid Berg were realized here; the cabin was home to them. They had bought the property, back taxes and all, from a woman struggling financially. This generosity carried them throughout their lives. The property on beautiful Borden Lake stretched before them and was a visual reminder of their native Sweden with its endless lakes.

The cabin boasted a tiny bedroom off the tiny but compact living room. The kitchen was a narrow walkway lined with cabinets, a toaster and a bread box on the counter. The kitchen table, painted green over wood, abutted the refrigerator. If you wanted to play a board game after dinner, the table was the happening place. It could hold four people comfortably, seven if you doubled up on an old wooden bench and brought chairs in from the living room. Off the living room was a set of treacherous, steep stairs that led up to the grand bedroom. In reality, this bedroom was an oversized loft. One might even venture to call it an attic. It had two windows, one on each end, to let out

47

the stifling summer heat, but the cure really would have been an air conditioner. The layout of the bedroom revealed wall-to-wall beds, all snugged up against each other. You had to duck your head when you made up the beds or risk smacking it on the low eaves of the room. At one time, there had been a woodstove in the living room to heat it in the chilly fall and bitter-cold winter, but that had been removed when the chimney was deemed unfit. The most essential room of all was not even *in* the tiny cabin; the outhouse was located "over the hill and into the woods," about a hundred feet from the back door.

I quickly learned that routine and tradition went hand in hand up at the cabin the first summer my husband and I visited the family in Minnesota. There were clearly defined gender roles at the cabin that had not wavered for many years. For example, upon arrival, the women (Loren's sister, his mom, and her Auntie Astrid) unloaded the car and went about setting up the kitchen. The old fridge had to be turned on, groceries were put away, and coffee needed to be made. Mousetraps needed to be disposed of out back. Rope was found and strung up outside to hang towels and bathing suits on after a dip in the lake. The men (my husband and his dad—Gust had passed away many years earlier) made sure that the gas tank was full and turned on. They checked the small, musty basement to dig out the hose that would connect the cabin to water.

Years before, a "sand point" pipe had been used. This was a hollow pipe sunk into the sand along the shoreline. The pipe would fill with water, and since it was somewhat filtered, it served as water to wash dishes in—but the rinse water was boiled first. The pipe was protected in a four-by-four-foot pump house. The water had to be lugged up to the cabin in buckets—a task my husband's sister and her cousin loved to do as kids. Later, when Loren's Uncle Curt built a modern house next door, the water hose was hooked up to an underground hose from Uncle Curt's well, making everyone's life so much easier at the rustic cabin.

The basement also contained inner tubes and blow-up toys, long since deflated over the winter. These were dragged out to be washed and aired out on the lawn. Later, a tire pump would be used to restore the inflatables to their original fun. The outhouse was checked to be sure there was toilet paper—kept in an empty plastic coffee can so the mice wouldn't eat it. The outhouse also needed to be swept out. Giant cobwebs of elusive spiders needed to be removed before anyone would sit on one of two "thrones." The final job of the men was to open up the old garage behind the cabin. This was the *agora* of the Swedes—the men changed clothes here, gathered here for fishing conversations, and dug out the mosquito fogger.

I was both appalled and fascinated by this stereotypical role-playing. I considered myself a modern woman. Couldn't I hook up the hose, inflate the inner tube, and sweep out the outhouse? (Not that I coveted this last job.) But there was something comforting and familiar about the routine of this. No one in Loren's family seemed upset by it. They were happy. They knew their roles here at the cabin and for them it was OK. I was assigned the job of making the beds upstairs. (Women's work, right?) Linens had been brought from home. There were cabinets at the top of the stairs with carefully wrapped quilts stacked in them if the night was chilly. As I tackled my bed duties, I wondered how Auntie Astrid, who was in her eighties, was going to get up those steep stairs. I selfishly assumed that my husband and I would get the bedroom downstairs; I still considered us newlyweds, as we had been married for only six months. I really didn't know Loren's family that well yet, but surely, they didn't expect us to sleep in the communal bedroom upstairs, did they?

As I pondered this, I could smell the aroma of coffee wafting up the stairs, but I also smelled something else; I couldn't place it. It was a sweet, heavy smell. I looked out the window just then to see my father-in-law walking the perimeter of the property waving a canister of something back and forth. A huge thick white cloud billowed out of the canister. I realized then that it was a chemical mosquito fogger. I feared for my unborn children at that moment. I finished making up the last bed and decided to take a quick trip over the hill to the outhouse to escape the lethal fog bank. When I stepped outside, I fully understood why the mosquito fogger had been deployed. As I walked toward the woods and the outhouse, a sudden swarm of mosquitoes surrounded me. I felt like the victim of a million vampires. On the run, slapping wildly at my arms, my legs, and my head, I flung open the outhouse door and was greeted by another cloud of mosquito repellant *whooshing* out. I had to make a decision: Do I die from chemical inhalation or from a million attacking mosquitoes? I chose Option #1.

I jumped into the outhouse and slammed the door shut. As I sat down on one of the "thrones," I heard the mosquitoes buzzing angrily outside the door. I tried to hold my breath so as not to inhale chemicals, but that was ridiculous. I was too busy swatting a few hardy mosquitoes that had not yet met their fate. Spying a few cobwebs way up high, I started worrying that a spider would crawl across my exposed derriere (which had actually happened to me in an outhouse in Maine—I'm still scarred by that experience...). As I prepared to employ the toilet paper from the coffee can, I heard footsteps. "Are you done in there?" It was my husband.

I could see that: 1. The mosquitoes and potential spiders were going to make me very efficient on the throne; 2. a lot of people were going to be using this outhouse; and 3. this was not going to be an easy trek if you had to pee or do something more serious in the middle of the night. I opened the outhouse door and made a mad dash back to the cabin, barely acknowledging Loren as I hustled along the wooded path. As I stepped through the back door, my mother-in-law greeted me with, "There's a washbowl on the table outside with some soap to wash your hands in." Outside? I had to go back outside? In Mosquitoville? I dutifully turned and ran as fast as I could to the washbowl. The familiar hum of those darling little critters was all around me, buzzing in my ears. I zipped back inside. Loren's sister was laughing. "You know the Minnesota state bird is the mosquito, don't you?" she said, handing me a flyswatter.

Fortunately, it was time for an afternoon delight. Food, that is. Auntie Astrid had made her special eggshell coffee. This was a new tradition for me. Astrid would mix a whole egg directly into the coffee grounds. Reportedly, it clarified the coffee and made it smooth. (Thankfully, it was boiled to kill any bacteria!) Buttery cookies were displayed on a large plate. The men were called in from the Great

Buggy Outdoors, and we all gathered around the table. Now this was a tradition I could get used to, although I wondered if my shorts would fit me at the end of the weekend. Life was good.

A short time later, the men and Auntie Astrid rose from the table. "Time for fishing," Astrid said in her musical, lighthearted voice. Fishing? Outside? It was almost dusk. Weren't bugs supposed to be worse in the early evening? Auntie Astrid disappeared into the tiny bedroom. She drew a curtain across the opening; this was her only door. There was a sudden realization that the bedroom was hers, which meant that Loren and I would be sleeping upstairs with his mom and dad and his sister. I smiled weakly at my husband, who seemed oblivious to my worries about mosquitoes and sleeping arrangements. Astrid came out of the room then. I nearly fell over. The sweet little old lady who had served us coffee in gilded cups back in Minneapolis last Christmas, whose home was decorated with glittering crystal chandeliers and beautifully hand-painted lamps, was dressed in an outfit that one could only describe as appropriate for the cover woman of *Fishing Digest*. Over her flowered dress, Astrid had pulled on a pair of blue cotton pants. (The dress was Astrid's signature style; she always wore one, no matter the occasion.) On top, she wore a blue cotton jacket, and there was a heavier version for colder weather on a hook in the hallway. A pair of rubber boots that came to mid-calf guaranteed dry feet. Topping it all off was her hat. Partly red-colored, partly netting, it had a wide brim. The flap of the brim could conceal the face when the sun was too strong or turn upward to expose the face on an overcast day. On this day, Astrid chose to turn it upward. The effect was Rebecca of Sunnybrook Farm Gone Fishing.

A long fishing rod in her hands, Astrid nodded to us and said, "Ready to go?" She smiled.

Everyone scattered and grabbed their sweatshirts. Bug dope was dispensed. I wanted to be a good sport, but I was dreading the excursion mainly because I didn't want to fight the bugs, but I also hated worms and squirmy things, and I knew they would be part of the fishing. My husband gave me a squeeze as we all trooped out to the boat, which was actually Uncle Curt's. It was a big, shiny new pontoon boat. I had never ridden in one before. Loren's dad was the captain; he started up the engine as we all found a seat to park in. The engine purred; the ride was smooth. As we backed away from the dock, I looked at the water. Borden Lake was glassy. Lily pads dotted the lake here and there, spiky pink flowers jutting up from their green cushions. There was a small island directly in front of us, and Loren recalled how he and his cousin had dared to swim to the island and back one summer when they were kids.

Everyone grew quiet then as they prepared their fishing hooks. Everyone except me, that is. I felt embarrassed that I was the *only* one out of the entire family who didn't want to pierce a wiggling, live creature on a hook. No one gave me a hard time; they just got down to the business of fishing. I could smell the Deet insect repellant all around us, but at least the mosquitoes had retreated to the surface of the lake. Occasionally, you could hear the soft *plop* of a fish surfacing, leaving rings of water ebbing out like the rings of an old tree. No one flinched. It was still and beautiful. Eventually, Auntie Astrid caught the first fish, which wasn't surprising since she had three different lines going at once. Apparently, this was no longer legal. "The warden warned me," she said, a bit naughtily. Everyone clapped when she reeled in her first catch of the day. It was a "sunny" she told me as she dropped the small, flat fish into a bucket. I watched it flop around helplessly. You are doomed, little fish, I thought. After a while, my father-in-law started up the engine, and we moved to a new location behind the island. It was here that I saw the eagle's nest high up in a dead tree along the shoreline. "The babies are still in the nest," whispered Loren's sister, handing me the binoculars. "Here, take a look." I couldn't believe my eyes. Several homely little birds with very pronounced beaks were wobbling just above the rim of the nest. No parents in sight, but it was fantastic to see these struggling wild creatures.

Soon after that, we hit a run of "sunnies"—everyone started catching them from the depths of the weeds in our chosen spot. We finally headed back home, buckets rattling with flopping fish. The sun's fiery red glow almost blinded us on the horizon and sent rays of reds and purples along the lake. I was transfixed, mosquitoes and all. When we got back to the dock, everyone seemed chipper. It had been a successful run. Auntie Astrid and the men headed to the fish house, and my mother-in-law explained that now the hard work would start. The fish needed to be cleaned, and again, everyone had a role to play. There was scaling, gutting, and chopping off fish heads. It was an assembly-line production. How wonderful, I thought, that Astrid was part of that. She broke female stereotypes on this one, but even I, a so-called modern woman, could not bring myself to help out in the fish palace.

After a dinner of fried sunnies (very bony but delicious!), tradition called for a game of rummy. Now this I could do. My husband's family was as serious about this card game as they were about fishing. Score pads came out, pencils got sharpened, cards were shuffled. We scrunched together around the table. A few stray mosquitoes were swatted, cookies appeared, and glasses of cold milk were served. After an hour or so of fierce competition, Auntie Astrid announced it was time for bed. "*Taks so mikket*," she said in her Swedish lilt. "Thanks for everything." We all helped clean off the table and put away the food, and the men suddenly disappeared outside.

"Better go to the bathroom now," Loren's sister told me, "else you'll have to go to the outhouse." She grabbed a flashlight and handed it to me. "Toilet paper is around the corner in the pantry."

What? And then it hit me. We didn't have to go all the way to the outhouse. We could step away from the house and tinkle at the edge of the woods. As I stepped out, I saw several flashlights bobbing in the darkness. Everyone had the same idea. Peeing with a flashlight in hand is really an art, especially when it's dark. Then there's the delicate matter of squatting and not peeing on yourself. Of course, the mosquitoes don't really care what you're trying to do—they just smell fresh, smooth skin and are all over it—literally. I finished this nightly ritual in record time. A combination of wiping, swatting, and yanking up my shorts while holding the flashlight (in my case, I just threw it on the ground) was pure circus. I was just thankful it was dark.

We all trooped up the stairs after our "nature walk." It was apparent we were all going to spend the night together in the loft upstairs:

my husband's mother, father, sister, he and I. All of us. It was about a hundred degrees up there. No need for any sheets or blankets. Loren's mom gestured for us to take the double bed up front near the window. His sister would be in the bed right next to us, his mom and dad in the bed to the rear of the room. All lights went out then. There were some muffled sounds as people got out of their clothes and into their nighties. A fan was turned on at the opposite end of the room from our bed; I doubted it would be very helpful. At this point, I was frustrated and afraid to move. I realized how much I liked my privacy and also how blasted hot it was in this room. Who could sleep? My husband, of course—he had fallen asleep immediately. His snore was loud and clear. I didn't dare breathe. What if I passed gas? Before long, there were more choruses of snoring. I couldn't tell if it was Loren's sister, his mother, or his dad. It sounded like more than one person. I lay still in the oppressive heat and darkness. Didn't this family have any sense of privacy? This was not a tradition I embraced.

As I lay there, I thought, what happens if I have to go to the bathroom in the middle of the night? My stomach was prone to terrible disturbances whenever I was nervous or upset. At that moment, I saw a flash of light at the end of the room. Following that, I heard a shuffle that sounded like someone dragging tin, and then I heard it distinctly: someone was peeing. It sounded like Niagara Falls in the silence. There was a giggle then. It was my father-in-law. "Success?" he said, laughing. "Oh, you—honestly!" my mother-in-law replied, laughing too. "Yes, success."

I wasn't laughing. It was all well and good that there was a chamber pot under *her* bed. I wasn't about to get up and try to use it, much less try to find it in the dark without waking anyone up.

Sometime that night I fell asleep. I woke in the early dawn hours to a most unusual sound. It was crystal clear and lilting, and it seemed to be coming from the lake. I slid out of bed—the others were still fast asleep—and looked out the window. I saw Auntie Astrid in a small rowboat, pulling the oars through Borden Lake as if she were fifteen. And she was singing:

Up at the Cabin

Sover sott, min lilla van,
Mama com er snort e yen...
Sleep sweetly, my little friend,
Mama is coming soon again...

I couldn't make out her face; I didn't have to. Every note rang true and clear. She was unencumbered; she was free; she emanated pure joy. On the lake, dressed in her fishing gear, she was in her element. I knew she would come in eventually. She was the Queen of the Swedish Pancakes. She always mixed up the batter and let it rest while she went out fishing. Loren had often talked about how he and his cousins always competed to see who could eat the most pancakes. Suddenly, it didn't seem so important that I have a private room or an air conditioner. This cabin, this tiny stucco cabin, was a house of memories for Astrid. This is where she and Gust had spent many moments together, fishing, cooking Swedish pancakes, and swimming in the smooth waters of Borden Lake. Gust was gone now, yet her song echoed mightily across the morning on the lake. I looked down at my snoring husband and smiled. I was lucky he was still beside me. We had a lot more memories to make together.

On Vacation

Minnesota Madness

I was fully prepared for the blast of cold that awaited me that Christmas. I was headed for the Midwest—Minnesota in particular—and I knew what to expect. Bitter cold in the winter and hot and unbearably humid in the summer. Why did people want to live there, anyway?

I knew I could handle the arctic blast sweeping down from Canada—it was all over the news. I was from Maine and no stranger to cold winters. No, I wasn't worried about the bone-chilling cold; I was worried whether or not I would receive a frosty reception from my fiancé's family or be warmly welcomed as a future family member. I was as Irish as Loren was Swedish, and we both cherished our staunch holiday traditions. We were about to meld our two cultures under one Midwestern roof. I had heard all about the Swedish Christmas traditions from Loren. "Every inch of the house is decorated," he'd said, "and every inch has some sort of Swedish goat, ceramic *tomte* [the equivalent of an elf], or wooden plaque with phrases like 'Var so gud!'"—which meant "That was good!" in reference to food, of course. I thought about my family's Christmas tree that was put up on Christmas Eve—as a kid, it was excruciating waiting for that night—and I also recalled the heavy toasts to St. Nick that followed. That must have been the Irish part, right? My great-grandmother was born in Ireland and had spent a number of Christmases with us reliving her childhood. I was fascinated with her Irish brogue and wanted to imitate it so badly. I knew the jig would be up, though, if someone asked me where in Ireland I had grown up. My fiancé's family was the real deal: His mother and all the relatives on her side spoke fluent Swedish, and I was about to experience it all.

The plan was for me to fly out as soon as school vacation started, but Loren was leaving a week earlier. He was going to drive his truck out so that he could bring back some of his belongings, his most prized being his Austin Healy. He was going to tow it cross-country and back to Maine, and I would ride with him on the way home. The plan sounded good, but I hated flying at the time—in fact, I was terrified—and doing it alone was even less appealing. In spite of my stomach doing an anticipatory lurch, I marked the departure date on my calendar, and counted down the days.

As the day approached, so did the winter "Fates and Furies"; it started to snow and continued to snow heavily. All my family training in Irish superstitions surfaced: Wasn't this a bad omen that clearly meant I should not fly? I kept asking myself that question as I boarded the plane heading for Detroit, then on to Minnesota. It wasn't long before the pilot announced that—you guessed it—it was snowing heavily in Detroit. So heavily there was only one runway open and only one plane landing—that was us. The passengers quieted down and buckled up. We landed safely in spite of the weather and had a short layover. Once we took off again, I was so grateful to still be alive that I ordered a glass of wine. A lot of other passengers shared my sentiments. Soon everyone was friendly and chatting it up. You could feel the excitement throughout the plane. The holidays were coming! After a second round of wine, I opened up to the people sitting near me, and I remember telling them that I was going to marry a Swede and learn all about the Swedish Christmas traditions. Even with my Irish heritage rooting for me, the combination of wine, no food, and a raging snowstorm caught up with me. I did what any sane person would do: I fell asleep.

I awoke with the man next to me gently tugging on my sleeve and saying, "We're here. We're in Minnesota. We made it. Merry Christmas," he added as he got up to deplane. I couldn't believe it! I had slept for two hours! And we were safe and sound on the ground.

Yippee! I grabbed my belongings and shuffled out with the rest of the sleepy passengers.

I spotted my fiancé in the crowd—tall, blond, so handsome. I grinned and waved. He saw me, but his face wasn't smiling. A look of concern shadowed his face. Later, he would describe how I looked as I approached: a bedraggled waif, hair sticking up, lipstick smeared, and a giant wet spot on the collar of my shirt—oh, God, had I drooled, too? But his folks didn't react at all. They enveloped me in their arms, chatted about the weather, and asked how my plane ride had been. I smiled and tried to make conversation, but nothing coherent seemed to leave my lips. My fiancé whispered in my ear, "Celebrating the holidays already, my love? I missed you," he added, and hugged me close. We made our way to the baggage claim and then outside to the car. It was minus ten degrees and the wind was howling.

The next few days were a blur. We spent the days traveling, meeting relatives, eating food, meeting more relatives, and eating more food. I quickly surmised that the Swedes would never go hungry, especially during the holidays. I heard lilting Swedish all around me at family gatherings, but everyone was kind enough to speak to me in English or translate what was being said. They treated me like a goddess, but I knew that image would quickly fade if I continued with the same eating patterns for much longer. My fiancé's parents were delightful and never mentioned my Opening Night appearance. I did everything I could to be polite, help clean up after meals, and share acceptable stories about my job at school, and even some safe stories about my family. I was still nervous about meeting everyone, and I had to remind my stomach that all was OK. After all, I had survived two plane rides in a blinding snowstorm, hadn't I?

Christmas Eve was a couple of days after my arrival. My future mother-in-law explained that this was the most important holiday for the Swedish people other than Midsummer's Eve. Church was the foundation of this holiday, and my fiancé's family was devoutly Lutheran. We would be attending a church service and then traveling two hours to unite with all the family at Stan and Bernice Ahlquist's house. Stan was Auntie Astrid's grown-up nephew. Auntie Astrid held a place of honor in this family. Even in her eighties, she still fished up at Borden Lake in the summer and was the glue that bound the family together. She had come over from Sweden with her husband, Gust, years before. Gust had long since died, but the family had rallied around Astrid and marveled at her resilience. She radiated light to everyone she spoke to. I couldn't wait to meet her. A wave of nostalgia came over me as I thought about my own family, whom I had left behind this holiday. I thought about my great-grandmother, Nana. Astrid would surely fill that homesick hole in my heart. I was ready for some fun.

That Christmas Eve turned out to be one of the coldest in years. The minus ten degrees I had experienced at the airport had stayed constant. The wind howled bitterly. No one seemed to mind even as my own teeth chattered, but it wasn't a blizzard after all, my Swedish family explained. There was an added surprise when my fiancé's sister flew in from Arizona at the last minute. She was about ten years older than me, but we had an instant connection. Her long jean skirt, cowboy boots, and great sense of humor clinched it for me. I, too, had planned a special outfit for the evening—a red satin dress I had worn to a wedding. Everyone wore red around the holidays, didn't they? I had also brought my fake fur coat, anticipating the frigid weather. I was decked out and ready to party. We all piled into my fiancé's dad's car—a big old Buick with room enough for three adults in front and in back. The heater blasted feeble warmth on that frigidly cold winter night, but we were soon singing Christmas songs and warming up nicely as we huddled together. I was excited to meet the next round of relatives. I also heard stories of the upcoming Christmas Eve dinner—apparently, it was a seven-course event! I wondered if the seams on my red satin dress would burst after all that good food!

We picked up Auntie Astrid at her house on the way to church. A tiny ball of energy, Astrid took me in immediately as a member of the family and sat me down in a comfy living room chair to get better acquainted. She offered us all buttery Swedish cookies—*pepparkakor*, she called them—and coffee to keep us awake in church. Astrid's eyes twinkled knowingly as she gazed at my fiancé and me. She spoke a few words in Swedish to my fiancé's mother, who nodded and laughed. I knew they were sharing a moment about the new arrival from Maine—but I didn't dare ask.

The candlelit service at the church was beautiful, and afterwards, we headed to Stan and Bernice's. My head was spinning after introductions to so many people, all of whom showed kindness and unabashed curiosity about "Loren's girl from Maine." Just when I thought I might fall over from exhaustion, Stan winked at me and announced, "Time for dinner! Hope you're hungry!" I nodded politely, but I was still tasting the rich buttery flavor of Astrid's cookies.

We all gathered around several tables that had been pushed together. The colors of the foods, the beautiful red Christmas plates, and the festive colors everyone wore blended together in true Swedish Christmas spirit. The family delighted in telling me about each course as it arrived. This was a *smorgasbord*, they explained as the first course arrived at the table. "This is pickled herring," Stan said, pointing to the plate of what looked to me like fish that had just been thrown onto the boat. "Chunks of raw herring marinated for days in a special sauce. And here comes the *silta*, or jellied veal loaf, and the head cheese. It's not the brains of the animal, just those tender pieces of meat from the head area," he added, seeing the look of horror come over my face. "Oh, and look, we have delicious deviled eggs and pickled beets—yum!"

Everyone nodded in assent as Stan talked. All eyes seemed to be on me, so I dutifully put some of each thing on my plate. I pretended I was eating my great-grandmother's Irish soda bread as I ingested the squishy veal, the head cheese, and the deviled eggs (which were even suspect at this point). No sooner had I washed down the first course than the second appeared. Bernice put down an array of breads: flatbreads, hard, dry, and brittle, and *kaffebrod*—coffee bread. This was a labor of love because it took a full day to make it. This was Loren's mom's specialty, and she smiled sweetly at me as she handed me the plate of breads with red and green sugar sprinkled generously over the top. The flatbread was pretty bland, but the coffee bread was delicious. I asked what the aromatic spice was that I tasted in the bread and was told it was cardamom, a new taste for me. I sat back, feeling very full.

Then, all of a sudden, the *next* course was on its way from the kitchen. Plates of meatballs, brown-sugared beans, and thick slices of ham appeared from the never-ending Swedish kitchen. Everyone clapped and congratulated the cooks as they heartily dug into the feast before us. I was astounded that no one was crying at this point. My stomach was hurting already, and this was not even the main course. I entertained thoughts of ripping my dress off because it was so tight now, but the pass-the-plate ritual had begun. My plate was full again with new foods and tastes to sample. I took tiny bites of everything, and everything was delicious! I silently congratulated myself for still being alive after this round, but the best was yet to come.

As the plates of food were cleared from the table, conversation died down, and it seemed like there was a moment of somberness. Everyone looked to Loren's father. As if on cue, he turned to say to me solemnly, "The next course is the most important and the mainstay of the Swedes. Each year cod is caught, cleaned, and soaked in a brine of lye for several days."

Did I just hear the word *lye*? Wasn't that poisonous? I thought soap was made from that in the olden days… Before I could pick my chin up off the table, Loren's father continued, "Then it is hung up to dry until it gets hard as a rock."

"So hard it could knock someone out," another relative said, straight-faced.

Loren's dad went on, "Then it is reconstituted by soaking it several times in a water bath. After that it is baked like any regular fish."

Regular? Nothing about this fish sounded regular to me.

"LUTEFISK!!" everyone shouted in unison.

Bernice brought in a large platter at that moment and placed it triumphantly in the middle of the table. It looked like haddock but had a very shiny, gelatin-like appearance, I noticed. Jellied fish. I was about to eat jellied fish. Suddenly, a quivering piece was put on my plate. Was this really a serious ritual? I wondered, or was it some sort of Swedish hazing? Oh, where was my prime rib and Yorkshire pudding dripping in savory meat juices?

The whole family ate their fish with gusto, alternately shaking and nodding their heads at each other. Auntie Astrid leaned over to me then and whispered, "Everyone really *hates* lutefisk, but it's a tradition. Some years it's good; others, not so good." She winked at me and continued devouring the squirming fish. I brought a piece up to my mouth, popped it in, and everyone cheered. It took me about five minutes to swallow it.

Someone muttered, "*Uffdah!*" which was the universal slang for "Oh, no!" as the last course finally came: *risgrot*, or rice velling—a creamy rice pudding with more cardamom. The bowls were placed in front of us. This time, Loren's mom spoke. "You know, there's a tradition in Sweden. People say whoever gets the almond at the bottom of the rice bowl will be the next to marry." A howl of laughter went up at the table and I knew that the almond was waiting for me at the bottom of my bowl. I was touched by this family's warmth and caring. I gazed over at my fiancé with a loving smile.

It was about ten o'clock when we all piled into the old Buick to make the two-hour trip back home. I was exhausted from the tension of behaving myself and trying to make a good impression on Loren's family. I was also so full I had nearly passed out when yet another round of buttery cookies—*sandbekels*—had made their way to the table after the rice velling. I laid my sleepy head on my fiancé's shoulder. I was snuggled between him and his dad, who was driving. Auntie Astrid, Loren's sister, and my future mother-in-law were sandwiched in the back, and everyone was content to be quiet as we struck out for home. The heater hummed as we drove in silence. A soft snore—Astrid's—came from the backseat.

What a great night this had been! I was reliving the events, the people, and all that food when my stomach started a low growl. I looked around, but no one seemed to have heard it, or at least they paid no attention if they had. I tensed my muscles in an effort to stifle it. Another long, low growl immediately followed. This was not good. A wave of discomfort swept over me. I couldn't deny what was happening. I lifted my head and whispered to Loren, "I think we'd better find a place to stop. My stomach is acting up."

He looked at me like I had six heads. We were on a backcountry farm road—endless snowbanks on either side of us, an occasional farmhouse jutting up in the night—but no gas stations, restaurants, or convenience stores, only Minnesota stars and snowy roads. He pointed at the snowbanks and whispered back, "Can't you wait? We're in the middle of nowhere."

I looked at him with very large eyes, took a deep breath, and settled back into the seat, determined to ignore the growing pain in my belly. The silence lasted for a couple of minutes until an unearthly, primitive growl was heard. At this point, both Loren and his dad were looking at me as if to say, *What the heck was that?* I smiled weakly, took another breath. I prayed, pleading with God to make this go away. Oh, no! *Uffdah!* God help me! A new wave—an unmistakable one that spoke to me made me lean into Loren and whisper loudly, desperately:

"We have to STOP! NOW! STOP THE CAR! *ANYWHERE!*"

Suddenly, the backseat was wide awake. Loren's dad quickly swerved to the right and jammed the car into park beside a snowbank.

"LET ME *OUT*—NOW! *NOW!*" I screamed, as I clawed my way out of the car, a madwoman with a primitive growl that was now quite audible to everyone. I looked around, desperate, frantic, knowing that I must squat and squat quickly. Snowbanks were to the left and right of me lining the road. Instincts took over: Suddenly, I had superhuman Olympic abilities—I knew I could leap over that snowbank and get out of sight of the car if I just executed one giant leap—which I did.

Later, I could only imagine what the five people in the car witnessed that night. Visions of fur and red satin flying up around my derriere as I leapt. And as I leapt, I knew it was too late. A hot stream of diarrhea filled my pantyhose, but I kept going. As I ran down the other side of the bank, it just kept coming, oozing down the backs of my legs. I knew that *this* Cinderella had dropped a whole lot more than her shoe at the stroke of ten. I lost my balance on the icy snowbank and slid on my fanny the rest of the way down. I lay there for a moment, not knowing if I should laugh or cry. No one came down to help. There wasn't a sound on this freezing Christmas Eve night. I finally composed myself and yelled up to the car, which was barely visible over the snowbank, "Lorrrrren, you got any tissues?"

I heard the whir of the electric window of the Buick, and Loren yelled back, "We're sending my sister down to help you." After all, we weren't married, and this was a Lutheran family.

Loren's sister slid down a moment later and handed me the pile of tissues she had been delegated to deliver. We looked down at the tissues and then she burst into laughter. I did, too, as I lay in a warm pile of goo. In reality, I wanted to cry, but then we heard a noise. It was the sound of a tiny creek. There must have been a strong current, as it wasn't completely frozen over. She and I had the same thought.

"Take off your pantyhose," she said, "and throw them in the creek."

I managed to get them off. I would have been frozen, but the hot liquid provided warmth. She told me she was going back up for more tissues. I cleaned up the best I could, but my red satin dress and fake fur coat were no longer festive. Three trips later, the tissues did the trick. We were both freezing by this point, but we tried not to laugh as we climbed up over the snowbank. I quickly noticed that everyone had either moved to the front seat of the car or squeezed to the extreme sides of the backseat. Plenty of space for Miss Maine. I climbed in the car, thankful that no one could see my face in the dark. They didn't have to. They knew I was there by the smell. It was a long ride home in a heated car. Loren's mom cooed and clucked over me but stayed on her side of the car.

I threw the red satin dress away, but we did take the fake fur coat to the cleaner's the day after Christmas. Loren's mom had covered it in plastic and hung it in the cold garage in a special place. Imagine the expression of the dry cleaner man when he unwrapped it...

• • •

Yes, I did end up marrying Loren, even after all that. And his parents and sister came all the way to Maine for the wedding. His mother brought an extra box of tissues with her, just in case. His sister was a bridesmaid. She brought a loaf of *kaffebrod*, made with love. We married the day after Christmas, and there was no lutefisk in sight—anywhere. I have the utmost respect for the power of Christmas Eve traditions. And I know that sometimes those Irish omens are just a snowbank you need to climb over to get to the good stuff on the other side.

Beware of Grizzlies and RVs

2002 became the year of the trip out west. You know, the family adventure in the rented RV, but not the "mega-boat" version because neither Loren nor I could back it up easily. (He would object to this statement, of course.) No, we had the very homely, economy-size RV with a low-down bottle-nosed front that gave it the appearance of a duck's bill hovering over a pond. The living quarters boasted two mini couches across from each other that turned into beds behind the driving area. The kitchen or dining table magically collapsed and transformed into a bed, comfortable for someone about three feet tall. There was a mini fridge and a stove, and even an overhead closet to store maybe three cans of beans or two boxes of cereal in, take your pick.

In the back, away from the passengers, at least as far away as one could get in the economy-sized RV, was a bathroom. It was about the size of a child's closet with lovely curtains over the three-foot window for privacy. It even had a shower to the left of the toilet. My family and I were quick to observe that the act of taking a shower would require a background in gymnastics; it measured about two feet by two feet. We discussed campground showers immediately after our tour of our soon-to-be home away from home. Ben and Katy each claimed a couch, leaving my husband and me the only other sane alternative: the bunk bed over the cab of the vehicle. It had about five inches of space to breathe in—OK, maybe it was eight inches. Loren and I looked it over and decided we might be able to sleep together if—and I do mean *if*—we could squeeze ourselves in there. All in all, my family was pretty darned excited about our upcoming road trip.

We had flown from Maine to Minnesota to visit relatives. From there, we rented the RV. Our goal was to explore the West: Washington State, Montana, and Wyoming. Our first stop was Montana, home of vast, flat plains that boasted mountains to the west if you could just wait to get there. Miles of flat, open spaces led to many games of Fish and Crazy Eights. Board games came and went. Then the dreaded words all parents do not want to hear, EVER: "Are we there yet?" At long last, the Rockies loomed in the distance. They were impressive even from afar, and our spirits were renewed.

We had traveled all day and were heading to a nearby campground called Grizzly Pass. It was the closest campground off the highway, and we weren't picky because we were tired. As we drove into the campground, the headlights flashed on big signs saying, "BEWARE OF GRIZZLIES." Grizzlies? I forgot that we were indeed in the land of those big, furry, *dangerous animals.* I glanced nervously at my husband, who shrugged and waved me off. The kids saw the signs, too, but that didn't keep them from sleeping soundly that night (and why wouldn't they sleep well in those deluxe beds??). I did not sleep. I did not turn and toss, mostly because there was no room to do so in my cozy nook over the duck's bill, but Loren snored loudly next to me. I heard every crackle, every twig, every night owl, and I'm sure I heard the crashing of what had to be one of those grizzlies thrashing around our campsite during the night. My stomach growled in anxiety, and when I was anxious, it usually meant a quick trip to the bathroom. It was comforting to know that I could get to the bathroom in the RV if I really had to rather than going to the community bathroom at the campground, although the journey out of my bunk space and over my husband's body could be an adventure of its own. Over the kids and through the RV, to the bathroom I will go, I thought, in something of a nervous state. Miraculously, however, I fell fast asleep.

The next morning, I woke up to find that Loren was not in the RV, and I figured he must have gone for a walk to check out the campground. I executed a sliding roll out of my bunk, feeling a little stiff from the cramped space where I had slept. The kids were fast asleep on their comfy couches—they didn't even stir when I maneuvered around their pull-out beds. There was exactly two feet of space between their beds. Ha! I thought. No grizzly's gonna get me! I made my way to the bathroom, stepping over tossed clothes and sneakers. I closed the door of the bathroom for some semblance of privacy. As I started to sit down, there was a noise that sounded a lot like a car engine turning over. I realized as my derriere descended to the throne that yes, indeed, I was hearing a car engine, and it was *our* car engine. It was a surreal moment—me descending to the throne, and the RV lurching to a start and actually moving along the road. It was like a water-ski tow gone amuck. There was no grace in the way I fell back over behind the toilet, smashing my hip and casting my legs straight up in the air. I was firmly wedged behind the toilet exposing assorted goodies for all the world to see.

I screamed, of course, because the motion startled me, my hip hurt, and I was stuck. The scream woke my two darling children. They ran to the bathroom door and opened it, just in time to see their mother, legs in the air, wedged behind the toilet in a most unusual position. Loren had heard the scream, too, even though he was down in the bowels of the RV. He slammed to a halt and crawled up from the driver's seat to see who was hurt. Three pairs of eyes stared at me for, oh, I don't know—two seconds.

"Awww, Mom," Ben groaned, embarrassed by Anatomy 101 class right before his eyes.

"Mom, are you hurt?" Katy piped up, oblivious to my anatomy on full display.

My husband just burst out laughing. Then he gave me a pull up and out of the corner of the petite bathroom. His intentions had been honorable, he told me. He thought he would get a head start on the road and let me sleep off the grizzly bear dreams... As for my kids, it would be years before they told anyone what "lesson" they had learned from their mom on a cool morning in the mountains of Montana.

Geckoes in Mexico

April was the perfect time for a vacation in sunny Mexico. Living in the state of Maine year-round makes you appreciate any and every day over seventy degrees. Winter in Maine announces itself in late November and sticks around like an unwanted guest; it isn't until sometime in mid-May that you are convinced there is more than one season in the state. So when my husband announced to the kids and me right before April school vacation that it was time to get away from it all, Katy and I started jumping up and down with excitement. Ben played it cool—he didn't say much—he was, after all, in high school. And why not Mexico? my husband suggested. Land of sunny, warm days and turquoise waters, delicious fresh seafood, and Margaritas the size of a quart of milk. And then there was the live music—salsa dancing that even the kids would get into. Who wouldn't want to go? I was teaching elementary school at the time. Ben was fifteen and Katy, thirteen. We knew it wouldn't be long before neither of them would want to be seen with us, especially in the tropics of Mexico, so we thought this might be our last hurrah for a while.

The day of our flight approached. Our suitcases were filled with crisp new shorts, T-shirts in all colors, flip-flops, and an assortment of bathing suits. We were going to fly to San Antonio as our first stop, then to Cancun, and by taxi and ferry twenty miles out to a tiny island called Isla Mujeres—Island of the Women. According to a legend, the island was named after the Mayan goddess Ixchel. She represented the moon, fertility, and happiness. Clay statues of her and her priestesses had been found all over the island, hence the name. Reportedly, it was beautiful there and we would not be disappointed.

As our plane descended, there were gasps of delight as passengers oohed and aahed at the sparkling waters beneath us. Suddenly, our plane took a right turn and pointed its nose at an angle I would have termed almost vertical. I noticed there were mountains on either side of the runway. I clutched my husband's arm tightly as we did a fancy dance toward the runway. Was it just me, or was that a hairy maneuver the pilot had just executed? I looked over at my kids; my son was sleeping, and my daughter was gazing out the window—no anxiety in sight. None of the other passengers seemed to mind the abrupt landing, so I looked at Loren again to see his reaction. He was looking out the window and smiling. Okey-dokey, I thought. Get over your plane paranoia.

We could feel the intense heat of the tropics as soon as we stepped outside. We were instantly bombarded with another language, another culture, and some pretty atypical-looking taxicabs. Several people approached us at once, asking where we were going and if we wanted a ride. My husband finally selected one of the men standing near us. As soon as he did, the others skulked away, disappointed. "Isla Mujeres ferry, please," my husband said in plain English. None of us spoke fluent Spanish, although my kids had several years of it from school. The taxi driver nodded, took our suitcases, and we piled into an old beat-up taxi that looked like it had taken the last passengers to the Neverlands. I had a worry pit of fear in my stomach, but Loren was quiet, and the kids didn't seem to mind at all. I shouldn't have worried; it was all a blur. The twenty miles to the ferry, which included driving past the tourist resorts of Cancun, went by at lightning speed. The taxi driver tried to make small talk in broken English, but I was just hoping he would slow down, just a little. From the backseat, the speedometer showed 88 miles an hour, and the meter ticked continuously and clicked as each new dollar rolled over on the screen, reminding us of how far we were from civilization.

Palm trees, looking dry and parched, swayed in the breezes as we swept by. What the heck had we gotten into? For all I knew, this taxi driver could be taking us to the nearest cartel. Just when I thought our lives might be in danger, the terrain changed. Small, colorful shacks lined the streets, and then we saw more turquoise waters. We pulled up to a dock. People were everywhere—natives, tourists, children, cats and dogs, all in a crowded throng. Lining the plank to the ferry was an assortment of native men, who leaned against the ropes of the railing, smiling with yellowed teeth; some wore cowboy-style hats. It was like a scene from a stereotyped movie. As we dragged our suitcases to the ferry, we felt their eyes on us, gauging us, inspecting us. And now we were going to go even further from civilization.

Ben had come alive by that time; he ran ahead to get on the ferry and check it all out. As it turned out, we were all squished together inside the ferry cabin, which was extremely hot. No air conditioning anywhere. The Isla Mujeres gang crowded in with us. There wasn't a space to spare as the ferry pulled away from the dock. Then the fun began. We rolled and pitched as the small ferry plowed through each wave. Loren started looking a little green. He got up and went to a window. I noticed the smell of gasoline exhaust and also the smell of the chickens who were accompanying us in several cages scattered around the inside of the cabin. Both of my kids seemed to be taking in their surroundings; they were great adventurers, and nothing fazed them. I smiled cautiously at the woman next to me. She returned my smile with a big toothy grin.

When we reached the island, our moods changed instantly. It was paradise. The water everywhere; the beautiful pink-toned houses, beaches, and sand; the narrow quaint streets. We were excited and delighted. Using our map, my husband steered us on foot down several streets toward our hotel. We lugged our suitcases behind us, anxious to get there. The hotel wasn't fancy, but you could see the water, and it was scrupulously clean. I was finally relaxing—that is, until the concierge reminded us about the toilet use: We would have to throw our soiled toilet paper in the garbage can in our bathroom. Obviously, this man

75

did not know our family. There wouldn't be a garbage can big enough to accommodate our fiber output. The thought of putting used toilet paper in the garbage made me realize how good we had it back home.

We soon got over our hesitancy about the accommodations. The sandy beaches and warm waters called to us, and we headed for the beach. Ben and Katy immediately plunged into the water. My husband and I preferred to sit on the beach for a bit to gather our wits. It was then that I noticed an elderly gentleman heading for the water. Normally, I wouldn't have thought much about it except for one fact: he was buck naked. He was also smiling at us and oblivious to our mouths hanging open. We weren't prudes, but hey, shouldn't an elderly gentleman have enough wherewithal to at least wear a Speedo, for God's sake? The gentleman slid into the water and bobbed in the waves. I stole a glance at the kids. They must not have seen him. It wasn't long, though, before he emerged from the water and headed back up to a spot on the beach where his wife? girlfriend? sister? was sitting at a small table, her naked breasts dangling and bobbing in the hot sun.

Loren and I immediately looked at each other: Holy cow! Did we check into a nudist hotel? We looked around and saw that everyone else, all shapes and sizes, seemed to be wearing some sort of bathing suit. Phew! We laughed out loud then and mumbled something about "boy, the kids are going to get an education." My husband, relieved, got his snorkel mask on and then his flippers. He waded into the water. I took a quick dip to cool off, and it was wonderful! Crystal-clear waters.

We spent a couple of hours at the beach, then headed back to the hotel. Thinking we had escaped the nudist couple, my son remarked, "Oh, yeah, I saw those naked people." We stayed at that hotel for two days until Loren surprised us by relocating us to a lovely resort nearby. This place was much fancier. Tropical flowers abounded. Sidewalks were sculpted with gorgeous shrubbery. Dinner was served in an open-air restaurant where you could bury your toes in the sand—no shoes required. Mariachi bands played for the tourists on the beaches in front of the hotel—for a fee, of course. And best of all, waiters in bare feet ran up to you on the beach and asked if you would like another Margarita. We were living it up!

The kids spent the days swimming and snorkeling. Ben noticed the scooters that you could rent and use right on the beach if you wanted to. The minimum age was fifteen, so we relented. After all, he had his driving permit. What harm could it be if he stayed on the beaches? He was off like a shot and would be gone for an hour at a time. I did several repeats of frozen Margaritas and thought I was in heaven. My husband kept an eye on the kids. (Well, someone had to!) The last night before we returned home, we took the kids out to dinner at the fancy sand restaurant at the hotel. I indulged in salads, fresh fruits, and another frozen beverage. It was our last night, right? We had an excellent meal.

As we filed out to the main road, I felt something scratchy on my leg. I swatted at it, thinking it was a leaf or a twig. I had worn my silky white billowing pants with a long green silky tunic to beat the Mexican heat. The scratching didn't seem to go away. In fact, it seemed to be moving up my leg. I suddenly realized that there could be a *critter* crawling up my leg. I yelled, "Oh my God, there's something crawling up my leg!!" Everyone stopped in their tracks. "It's getting further up!" I screamed. I started jumping up and down in the sand (like that was going to make it stop...), and the kids looked at me like I was crazy— it's just Mom *reacting* again—but my husband had a simpler solution: "Drop 'em. Just drop your pants."

Normally, I would think this was a ploy on his part, but the kids were right there, and I was a desperate woman. Whatever it was, it was getting closer to an area that, well, shall we say, needed some protection... I could feel the scratching all over my leg. It was on a little vacation inside my pants leg. Where would it go next? With that thought, I obeyed Loren's command: I dropped 'em. The problem was, I forgot that I was going Caribbean style—Ms. Smarty Pants wasn't wearing any underpants. The kids gasped when they realized this as I stood in the middle of the road, jumping and screaming. Meanwhile, my cries for help had attracted the entire kitchen staff from the restaurant. They all lined up and clapped heartily. That did it. I took off running for our hotel room, tunic flapping in the wind, and something else flapping in the wind as well. The kids, who are grown now, like to tell it from their perspective: Mom's rear end clearly visible as she ran down the dusty dirt road to the hotel. It wasn't the first time they had witnessed a view of their mother's bottom on a vacation…

We left the next morning for the States, and we all had a story to tell when we got home. Katy would talk about how she got hookworm in the bottom of her foot, probably from waste in the sand; Ben would devilishly describe his scooter rides up and down the nearby nude beaches; and I would talk about my critter experience, which we think was a little gecko, based on the scratch marks on my leg. Loren would talk about *all* of these things. But the highlight for him had been his effort to track down something to stop my diarrhea from all the fresh fruits, salads, and Margaritas I had consumed. He was a miracle worker. He found the solution just before we boarded the plane. It was the Spanish version of Kaopectate.

Several years later, I related my gecko story to a group of teachers on a tour bus to Boston. My husband quipped, "Wish I had a suitcase full of geckoes!"

Badlands/Good Times

Every spring and summer school vacation, my husband, two kids, and I would pick a destination in the US where we would spend our vacation. When the kids were about nine and twelve, we thought it would be a great idea to do the South Dakota circuit: Mt. Rushmore, the Black Hills, and Badlands National Park. As a teacher, I immediately began researching these destinations to get the scoop on the best places to see, stay, and explore. I was familiar with Mt. Rushmore—not because I had been there, but because I had taught it at school as part of a unit on presidents. I was more interested in learning about the Black Hills and Badlands National Park. I have to admit I was a bit reticent about staying in an unfamiliar place called the *Badlands*. Sure enough, my research revealed that the origin of the name came from the Lakota Native Americans, who had dubbed it *mako sica*, bad land. It had everything to do with the lack of water there, the extreme temperatures, and the rugged terrain. Good grief, I thought, why would anyone want to stay there?

It was the rugged terrain that captivated visitors, however. Years of drainage from the three nearby rivers—the White, the Cheyenne, and the Bad (there's that name again) had eroded the layered or sedimentary rock formations into breathtaking colorful striations and stalagmite-like pinnacle rock formations. Now *that* sounded intriguing to me. Further research showed that there were only two major campgrounds in this park—the Cedar Pass Campground and the Sage

Creek Campground. The latter sounded primitive and too challenging for a family of four used to the comforts of home. I took the plunge and made a reservation at Cedar Pass. We were ready for our new adventure.

We drove from Maine to South Dakota over several days in our trusty family-oriented Caravan. We stayed in hotels along the way, saving our camping fun for the state of South Dakota. The van was packed to the roof with camping supplies, board games, coolers of food and ice, and our big orange tent that could really sleep eight people, not just four, comfortably. Sleeping bags doubled as pillows for the kids, who were sandwiched in the second seat. In the very back was our camping grill and a bottle of liquid fuel. (I admit I was a little nervous having *that* in the car.) Since the dryness of the Badlands prohibited fires, I was disappointed there wouldn't be any s'mores to indulge in, but I had remedied that by baking some yummy cookies.

The day we entered the park, it was evident we needed air conditioning. The thermometer in the car told us it was ninety-five degrees outside. It was a dry heat, not humid, but I was still thankful we could get some relief inside the car. As we drove into the campground, we took in our surroundings. Mountains of layered rock encircled the campground. It resembled a miniature Grand Canyon. At the base of the mountains was a flat, barren—and ugly—wasteland. The contrast was striking. Interspersed and random, single spears of rock jutted up from the barren floor of the campground. We could have been on another planet. At each campsite, a picnic table with a slatted wooden structure over it suggested shade was important here.

As soon as we stepped out of the car, the heat hit us full-force. It was excruciatingly hot, to say the least, and coming from Maine, it was a shock. It was easily a hundred degrees at our campsite, and we still had to set up our tent. Loren, ever positive, set to work and told us it wouldn't take long if we all worked together. That was the problem, however. The two of us had different ideas on how to put the tent together. Tired, hungry, and unbearably hot, I snapped. "Do it yourself, then!" I yelled at him, like a two-year-old having a tantrum. The kids just stood back, waiting to see what would happen next. "I'm going to the bathroom," I said, stomping off in the direction of a huge concrete building that stood about thirty feet from our campsite. Embarrassed by my behavior but miserable in the heat, I trudged on toward the bathroom. As I neared it, a sign caught my eye: "Stay on the boardwalk. Beware of rattlesnakes." I nearly peed my pants right then and there. *Rattlesnakes?* Of course, I had read about them in my research, but what did this mean? Were they lurking in the grassy area around the boardwalk, waiting to wave their hissy tails and strike at you as you passed? I scanned the area around the boardwalk as I hurried on.

The bathroom looked like a concrete fortress plunked in the middle of a desert. There were no windows in it, which I thought was odd. Inside, the concrete decor continued, but it was clean. I splashed water on my face. Other women wandered in, looking as hot and bedraggled as I did. We smiled and talked about the heat. By the time I returned to the campsite, the big orange tent-mansion was upright and ready for guests. The kids smiled at me. Loren came over and hugged me. "See? No problem," he teased. "Now, let's have some supper." Supper included a glass of wine for me, and I began to relax a little. We watched the sun go down over the wide expanse of mountains and flatlands. The smell of another camper's food wafted over us. Stars came out and the campground was transformed into an astronomical delight. Millions of stars were luminous in the crystal-clear night sky. You wanted to reach up and touch them. We forgot about the oppressive heat of the day. In fact, it was cooling off rapidly. We were tired and ready for our cozy sleeping-bag beds. We crawled into the spacious tent, grabbing a flashlight each, and snuggled into our sleeping bags. I could see the stars through the screened window at the top of the tent. It's beautiful here, I thought, as I drifted off to sleep.

Sometime later I awoke. I listened to the loud snoring of my husband and the softer breathing of my two kids lying near me. But there was something else I noticed: the wind. I could hear it distinctly. The loose flaps on the sides of the tent windows were smacking up against the tent. I looked up to the roof of the tent; the stars were no longer visible. As I lay there, I could swear that the wind was picking up even more. I began to feel that little pit of worry seep into my stomach. I turned toward Loren and said, "Loren, Loren, the wind is getting stronger." What an absurd thing to say to someone in a dead sleep, but I felt better just saying it aloud.

I turned back over and looked at the top of the tent again. Was it my imagination, or was the wind picking up even more? This time, I shook my husband's arm until he mumbled, "What? Er, what?"

"Loren, wake up! I think a storm's coming."

At this point, the sides of the tent began to expand and contract in rhythm with the wind.

"Hmmm, go to sleep," Loren murmured and turned over.

And at that moment, the sides and top of the tent began to shake violently. By this time, I was sitting up in a full state of panic. "Wake up! Wake up!" I yelled to my family over the wind. All of a sudden, the tent lurched violently and toppled, the roof of the tent covering us. We were being smothered by our tent. Everyone was awake now. I yelled, "Get out of the tent! Get out now!"

My husband, fully awake, switched on his flashlight, found the flap of the door, and unzipped it. "C'mon, kids, we have to get out of the tent," he said calmly.

We scrambled through the door, leaving sleeping bags behind. Once outside, it was like we had entered the Twilight Zone. I had never experienced wind like this. It was a full-force gale. The kids and I clung to each other. Loren disappeared behind the tent and into the darkness. Where was he going? I shrieked his name in panic. It seemed like hours, but minutes later he came into view. "I had to go pee!" he yelled over the wind. "Man, you should have seen it! The wind carried my pee in an arc—"

Really? He was extolling the virtues of wind and pee?? I thought we were going to be carried away. "Get the ranger!" I screamed at him, in full panic mode. "Find the ranger! We need help!" I hollered as my hair whipped and stung my face.

"The ranger is in bed," my husband shot back, in an attempt to calm me down. "He can't help us right now!"

Then the heavens opened up. It began to rain—not *just* rain, but *torrents* of rain. Buckets of rain. The kids screeched because they were getting soaked. "Get in the car," my husband ordered.

As I stood there in the rain, the previously beautiful sky turned into a demonic light show. Lightning forked down the sides of the layered mountains. I had never seen such magnificent or terrifying lightning bolts all at once, and I was rooted to the ground. I couldn't move. I was frozen in awe. As I watched, the forks of lightning wreaked havoc all around the rim of the canyon. At one point, a flash of lightning contacted the ground and exploded. We're in the bottom of a fishbowl, I remember thinking. Suddenly, my son, appearing out of nowhere, grabbed my hand and said, "C'mon, Mom, get in the car." And he led me as if I were the child to the safety of the Caravan. I climbed in front.

"Quite a light show," my husband said, squeezing my hand and promptly falling asleep.

I couldn't believe it. How could he sleep at a time like this? I turned to check on the kids in the second seat; they had already fallen asleep, too. The car began to rock in the wind and rain. I sat, staring and terrified, at the spectacle outside. I buckled my seat belt. I clutched the side arm of my seat. If we were going to be airborne, at least I would be secured to the car. Needless to say, I didn't sleep that night.

Sometime during the early hours of daylight, the storm subsided. I was wide-eyed, and my nerves were shot. I looked out my side window. I couldn't believe what I saw: There were tents down everywhere! They lay in disastrous heaps on the ground and over the picnic tables; some had been blown toward the bathroom. People were getting out of their cars. At least those had held fast. I opened the car door and crawled out, stiff from my upright all-night vigil. My family was still sound asleep, much to my annoyance. I made my way to the bathroom, ever cognizant of the potential rattlesnake threat, and was met with another shock. There were bodies all over the bathroom floor! Some had sleeping bags, others had blankets thrown over them. What the—? One woman stirred, then, and sat up. "Wow, that was some storm," she said, smiling at me.

"I'll say," I replied. "I didn't sleep at all. Our tent collapsed."

"Oh, you should have come in here," she said. "It's really safe. It's like a fallout shelter. It's the safest place to be when those tornadoes come whipping across the plain in the campground."

"Tornadoes?" I mumbled, still in shock.

"Oh, sure, they have them all the time around here. You know—heat during the day, cold at night. It's the perfect combo. Didn't you read the brochure?"

Apparently, I had not secured a brochure in spite of my research.

We packed up our campsite that day, wet tent and all. We were headed for a lovely hotel some miles outside of the park for the night. In a warm, safe bed. Maybe then, good times would be had by all.

Ride, Sally, Ride

Ireland.

    The name conjures up immediate images of green rolling hills, blue Irish seas, thick brogues, rocky walls surrounding castles of long-ago lore, and music—oh, the music! Fiddles that lament loves of the past. Who wouldn't jump at the chance to experience all that romance? That is precisely why I did not even hesitate when my longtime childhood friend invited Loren and me to go there with her and her husband for two weeks one July. Not only were we going to Ireland, we were going to go in style: We would get to see the real Ireland through the eyes of an authentic resident. His name was Liam and his website for an "Irish Escapade" had been more than convincing to my girlfriend as she researched a place for us to go.

    The trip focused on the beautiful peninsula of Dingle, located in the southwestern part of the Emerald Isle. Every day for two weeks, a new adventure was planned, right down to the bed-and-breakfast we would stay in, the tour we would go on, and the restaurant or pub we would visit each evening. We packed all our outdoor gear, as this was to be an adventure in hiking, kayaking, bicycling, and horseback riding. No previous experience was needed, just a willingness and ability to try out a new and wonderful way to see the Irish countryside. The trip was also a special one to me because my friend and I had backpacked to Europe thirty years prior; this was a reunion to commemorate our travels through Europe. Since we had been confined to the mainland that summer and had never reached the United Kingdom, this was our way of rounding out that earlier trip. Of course, it was also a great excuse to see each other, since we lived far apart in the States.

The sun was rising as our plane taxied down the runway at the Shannon airport. Liam was there to greet us. We loaded up his van with our worldly possessions and climbed in, completely at the mercy of a man we had never met. For the next several days, our eyes feasted on the beauty of our surroundings. Dingle was nestled in a valley and surrounded by both mountains and sea—breathtaking views everywhere we looked. The food was hearty and plentiful, but we walked it off every day. Liam kept us hopping with hikes from the upper sheep pastures (we quickly learned to avoid the slippery sheep dung) to the vast stretches of sandy beaches along the shore, all the while giving us a history lesson of the area as we went.

We bicycled through Killarney Park, stopping at Ross Castle to rest. We kayaked in the Bay of Dingle and saw massive sea urchins clinging to cave walls. We marveled at the sheer expanses of the cliffs that rose above us, and we even got to see Fungi, a dolphin that had become a local legend of the bay. It was stimulating, physically exhausting, and pure fun. Our cheeks were rosy from the sea air as we witnessed endless rock walls and fuchsia hedges six feet tall that lined the paths through woods and along roadways. Our hair was damp with dew or mist from the rains that came and went each day, but we forged on, buoyed by the colorfully painted houses in the village of Dingle and by the ships that also boasted an array of colors as they bobbed in the harbor. It all seemed quite magical and unbelievable. I couldn't wait to tell everyone back home about our trip!

On one of our last days there, Liam explained that we would be going horseback riding. While most people would have envisioned these beautiful, powerful animals trotting along the sandy beaches with tails blowing in the wind, I had a completely different and visceral reaction. This was one part of the trip that filled me with apprehension. I had flashbacks to when I was ten years old and living in Virginia. I was in love with horses then. I had read every Black Stallion book by Walter Farley, and every horse book by Marguerite Henry. I desperately wanted a horse of my own, and more than that, I wanted to ride one. We lived in a suburb of Richmond, in a small town known as Varina. Just around the corner from us was a racetrack. My parents took me there occasionally to see a race.

Tailgating was the thing to do even back then. Families parked around the fence that encircled the track, and there was an endless array of picnic baskets and red-checked tablecloths spread over the tailgates of the cars, and you knew there was a container of potato salad somewhere in everyone's cooler. Thick slices of watermelon lay temptingly on paper plates. The smell of fried chicken permeated the air. All this was exciting enough for a ten-year-old, but the real excitement was the race. I remember vividly the thud of the horses' hooves just feet away from me as I stood near the fence; I could hear the heavy breathing of the horses and stood back as they kicked up dirt in their wake. These occasional visits to the racetrack only fueled my desire to ride like the wind on a horse of my own. My school principal, Mr. Ward, lived around the corner from me on the way to the racetrack, and he owned several horses. He had a daughter named Sandra who was in high school and would have had nothing to do with a little kid like me except for the fact that I made it a point to visit her frequently when I took off on my walks in the neighborhood. How I envied her as I watched her exercise her horses around the fenced-in field across from her house.

One day as she was leaving the horses to graze in the field, she noticed me hanging on the fence. I told her how much I wished I could ride one of her horses. "Really?" she said. "I guess you could ride Sally. She probably wouldn't mind." She pointed to the opposite side of the field, where I saw a majestic black horse, head down, munching on grass. My heart nearly came out of my throat. Could my dream finally be coming true?

Sandra grabbed a saddle from one of the fence rails, and I climbed over the fence and followed her to where Sally stood. Sally looked like she was at least twenty feet tall—at least to a little ten-year-old kid who had never ridden a horse a day in her life. "Sally's pretty old now, so she will be gentle with you," Sandra reassured me. She saddled Sally up, then helped me get my foot in the stirrup. Next thing I knew, I was up and over and sitting on a very big saddle. The ground seemed far away as I sat atop my equestrian throne. Sandra went around to the other side and secured my swinging foot in the second stirrup. She handed me the reins. "Say 'whoa' when you want her to stop and 'giddy-up' when you want her to go. Bye!"

My excitement suddenly gave way to trepidation. Sandra was walking off to go back to the house. She waved at me as she climbed over the fence. At that moment, Sally suddenly lifted up her head from her munching as if she realized that: 1. Someone was sitting on her back; 2. her mistress, Sandra, had just left; and 3. she had spotted some tastier looking grass about five feet away. Without so much as a "giddy-up," she began to walk toward the tastier patch of grass. I could feel her powerful muscles moving beneath me; it was exhilarating and terrifying all at once. I nearly fell off. She seemed completely unaware that I was on her back. I grabbed the reins up near her neck and decided to try out my new command skills.

"Whoa, whoa!" I said loudly. Sally was oblivious. She bent her head to continue eating. With this movement, I nearly slid over her head. Her coarse mane was in my face. I was hanging on for dear life. I did not want to admit defeat, but I remember an urge to cry for help. Where was Sandra? Who leaves a kid on a horse like that, anyway? Suddenly, Sally lifted her head—she seemed to be checking out something on the other side of the field. She swung her head around and paused. She must have sensed that the pesky little critter on her back was afraid, so she broke into a trot across the field.

I was clutching her neck, holding on for all I was worth, but I dropped the reins as I bounced hard all over the saddle. Complete terror set in. The horse was picking up speed. I was crying. I was sure I was going to die any second—or worse, fall off and get trampled by old, gentle Sally, who had somehow come back to life. Just when I thought my life was over, Sally slowed to a halt. She began munching on grass as if nothing unusual had transpired. I sat up tentatively and decided it was time for me to get off the horse. I shook my foot free of the right stirrup and leaned to the left to dismount. It wasn't pretty.

As I swung my right leg up and over, I fell to the ground. Luckily, my left foot came out of the stirrup. I rolled away from Sally, got up, and started running. I didn't look back, and I'm pretty sure Sally never even looked up from her eating…

So here I was, forty years later—older and wiser—about to go on a horseback ride—again. My friend and her husband had some experience riding horses, so they were quite thrilled at the prospect of our next adventure in Ireland. My husband had absolutely no experience and was a bit reluctant to try it, but he was a good sport and willing to give it a go. I was just praying none of the horses were named Sally. As it turned out, some other tourists would be joining us, and all in all, there were about twenty of us who met up at the stable. Liam had promised to pick us up in a couple of hours, so we had to make the best of it.

After finding some sweaty helmets and very stiff riding boots in the tack room, we wound our way to the rear of the barn where our trusty steeds awaited. The horses looked well-groomed but very tired—that is, all except one. At the end of the line, towering over the other horses, pranced a big black stallion. His impatience was obvious: He twisted and turned as if he were trying to wrench free from his reins, which were securely tied to a post. Two lovely Irish girls were talking to him in soothing tones. I had an immediate flashback to Sally—gentle Sally who turned out to have a will of her own. What would a horse like this do once a rider was on his back? I shuddered at the thought.

A moment later, we were all assigned our horses. "And you shall ride our dear Paddy," one of the Irish guides said in her lilting accent. She was gesturing toward Loren, a big strapping Swede who was an easy match for Paddy. Oh, boy, I thought. My husband walked forward, straight toward the stepladder used to mount the giant steed. The girls held tightly to Paddy's reins until Loren was securely seated atop the giant. The dislike between the two was instantaneous: Paddy snorted and tried to turn in a circle. Loren grabbed the reins and brought Paddy's head up quickly. I noticed beads of sweat forming on his face. "This'll be fun, honey," I called out to him. He gave me a look that would have made the dead rise from the crypt.

On Vacation

The horses knew the drill; they formed a caravan-style line as the two Irish girls mounted their horses and led us to the roadway. My friend was near the front of the line, her husband and I were somewhere in the middle, and my husband was at the back of the line. One of the girls trotted over near my husband—not surprisingly, as she had noticed Paddy's mood. They explained we would be riding along the road, then across sandy beaches (ah, there's that romantic notion again!), then along a creek bed, through a meadow, and back to a road at the end of our hour or so journey.

The first leg of the ride gave me hope. You could hear the gentle *clip-clop* of the horses' hooves on the paved road. I could hear Loren's voice calling to the Irish guide in the back. I could make out the words, "A little help would be appreciated." Unbeknownst to me at the time, Paddy had decided to show his Irish will by stopping at every hedge along the road to munch on the leaves. If my husband steered him to the left with the reins, the horse went to the right. I was busy just holding onto the reins and hoping I wouldn't fall off. I didn't dare to even turn in my saddle to see what was happening at the back of the line.

As we neared the ocean, where sandy beaches awaited us, the Irish girl at the front of the line stopped and announced that there was a fence in the meadow section of the ride. "There are other horses fenced in by the meadow. Be careful, then, to keep your horse from wandering over to the fence to meet them. It will be difficult to get them away from their so-called friends." Fence? I would deal with that later. One *clip-clop* at a time. The sandy beach was beautiful, and I would have appreciated the scenery a whole lot more if my horse had not suddenly stopped in its tracks. I immediately heard a chorus of "Whoas" (I remember how well *that* worked!), including my husband behind us, who repeated it a number of times. It seemed my horse, inspired by all the water of the ocean, had decided to urinate right then and there. This was a new sensation for me—not just the sound of it, which reminded me of Niagara Falls, but also the volume—it seemed like it could fill a small lake. The horses behind me waited patiently. One of the Irish girls broke ranks and came up beside me to check out the reason for the delay. "Oh," she said, "come along, then." My horse immediately lurched into action and began to walk in the line again.

It wasn't long before my horse began to nip at the rump of the horse in front of me, which was the one my girlfriend's husband was riding. Each time my horse did this, his horse would bolt forward. Like a bad game of dominoes, all the other horses in front would then step out of line and prance about nervously at the disruption. I tried pulling up on the reins, but my horse, Molasses (yet another deceiving name), had an emerging passive-aggressive streak. The nipping went on for several minutes. Fortunately, my friend's husband could control his horse. I gripped the reins and prayed once again that I would stay upright.

We soon left the beach and turned toward a gentle meadow. I relaxed a bit as I smelled the sweet grasses mixed in with the salty air. The sea breeze was not as noticeable now. It felt warmer. I could hear the Irish girl in the back saying, "Come along, then, Paddy. Come along!" every few minutes. I wanted to have sympathy for my husband, but it was every person for himself. I spied an interlocking wooden fence just ahead on the left of our trail. None of the riders spoke as we approached; it seemed like a funerary march to me. All was quiet until a series of whinnies and neighs began. I looked to the left and saw about six horses in the meadow behind the fence. Our dutiful line of steeds suddenly perked up. They responded with whinnies of their own. In fact, the fenced-in horses were so excited to see their "friends," they were galloping full tilt toward the fence to greet them. The warning from the Irish guide flitted through my head: "Don't let them go near the fence…the fence…the fence…"

Suddenly, my girlfriend's horse broke from the pack and headed to the fence. I could hear her calling to her horse and see her gripping the reins, but to no avail. The horse was determined to see its cronies, and nothing was going to stop it. The horse went to the fence and rubbed noses with another horse in greeting. One of the Irish guides trotted over and grabbed the reins of my friend's horse, and the horse was reluctantly led away. Several others tried to follow suit, but my horse seemed disinterested, and I was totally thankful for his lack of social graces. I looked down at my hands and noticed my knuckles were white. My hands hurt from gripping the reins so tightly, but I had survived—so far.

Our next hurdle was to wade through a small, winding shallow creek. Water eddied gently over smooth round rocks. It seemed easy enough. My girlfriend's horse, leading the way, took a step into the water and stopped. No amount of coaxing, rein tugging, or gentle nudges in its sides would move the horse. It was still mad because its playtime with friends had been quashed. My friend started laughing helplessly as each horse in the line strode by her and her mighty steed. I laughed nervously, too; it could be me next. Apparently, Paddy and Loren also did a fancy dance in the water. We were nearing the end of the "happy trails" ride and returning to hard paved roads.

The Irish guide at the front of the line stopped and cheerfully announced in her best brogue, "Well, then, what a fine journey we've had. Let's canter back to the stable. Here we go, then." She turned her horse and took off like a shot, and instantly, all the horses came to life. It was as if they had all received electric shock therapy. The meaning of *canter* was crystal clear even to me, the inexperienced horse-rider. Molasses, forgetting his name, bolted. I instinctively leaned over the saddle horn, clutching the reins and the coarse mane of hair, which I was spitting out of my mouth as we flew—no, *cantered*—back to the stable. My bottom bounced painfully in the saddle, and I had a Sally-déjà-vu moment. And then it was suddenly all over. We reached the stable, and the horses, on auto-pilot, slowed their gait to a walk. I sat up. Some of the other riders were staring at me. Let them scoff, I thought. I had survived, hadn't I?

The rest of the group trickled in, including my friend, who had finally convinced her mighty steed that some good hay was waiting back at the stable. About ten minutes later, Paddy, my husband, and the other Irish guide arrived. She was holding Paddy's reins. The look on Loren's face said it all: Get me off this monster! I was relieved that he had survived, too. The guide led them over to an outdoor stairway by the stable. She tied the reins to the stair rail and went into the tack room while Loren waited for her to bring back the stepladdder to dismount. But Paddy was not done with his tirade of the day. I watched in horror as he deliberately backed into the stairway several times, tangling up the stirrup and my husband's leg, which was about to be crushed. Several people who witnessed this yelled out to the guides, and my husband called out, "I need some HELP—here *now!*" Paddy kept up his back-and-forth dance until one of the guides quickly grabbed the reins and untangled Loren's leg.

We had lots to talk about on our way back to the B&B that afternoon! Seated safely in our van, securely buckled in, we tended to our saddle aches and pains and enjoyed the views. Sally, Molasses, and a black steed named Paddy had all given us adventures to remember.

Vets, Vignettes, and Doggie Treats

Willie Wonder-Boy

As a pet lover and owner, one expects that visits to the vet will be a natural part of life. Our household consisted of two cats and a dog. Jazz and Joe were our adorable cats—one pitch-black, the other a gray tiger. The two cats were not brothers. Jazz had wandered into a barn one day following a duck with her ducklings. Joe, also a kitten at the time, was part of a new litter. Mama cat had immediately adopted Jazz and fed him as one of her own. Joe and Jazz bonded and became inseparable. My husband's office manager owned the barn where all the drama took place, and she told us the two cats were a "package deal." I was delighted. We also had a dog named Willie, a chocolate lab/golden retriever mix. He was a beautiful golden color. He was also willful and stubborn combined with sweetness and gentleness, and Loren had assumed the role of the alpha male. Willie adored me but behaved better with my husband.

In spite of this, I was the chosen one to do vet duty one summer day because I was a teacher and had the freedom to come and go as I pleased. The three animals were all due for their shots, but Willie had been gnawing at a point on his paw. It had become raw and bleeding, and we wanted it looked at. I dug out the two cat carriers to transport Joe and Jazz, and Loren dug out a leash and a choker collar to use with Willie. Loren kissed me goodbye and said, "Good luck"—such a sweet sentiment as he took off for work in his truck.

No one announced to the cats or to Willie *where* they were going that morning, so how did they know? It took me twenty minutes to find them, first of all. Jazz, the more reticent of the two cats, was under the couch sleeping peacefully. Joe lay asleep outside on the deck railing—but he was really *pretending* to sleep, as birds were flying to and fro all around him at a nearby feeder. I got the carriers ready—doors open—all set to go. I scooped up Joe. He melted in my arms—that is, until he saw the cat carrier. Not only did he have nine lives, he must have had nine memories of previous vet visits. Did that lovely vet office smell still linger? He went from a pliable mass to a stiff accordion. You know how you try to place them inside the carrier face first? Well, Joe suddenly became the tiniest cat in the world. His entire body squished together. He planted his front paws firmly in the lip of the carrier and would not budge. At this point, I had to lift up his body and paws and give him a firm push. I snapped the door shut and was met by a loud, plaintive growl. Not a happy kitty.

The growl must have been some kind of warning communication, because Jazz was no longer under the couch. I found him crouching behind the washing machine, where he used to hide out as a shy kitten. He was very trusting and let me pick him up easily. But he knew. He went from being a gentle lamb to a raging lion. All four legs stuck out, claws exposed. He then clung to my arm, claws and all. I finally was able to pry him loose…why hadn't I thought of a peregrine glove for this event? I nudged him into the carrier and quickly shut the door. He began to mew in the most pitiful little voice. By this time, I felt I had fought two world wars, but Willie was still left to conquer.

He was about two years old at the time, but he was big—about 85 pounds—and he was outside roaming the yard. When he saw me with the leash and collar, he got very excited. He started racing around me in circles, stopping once in a while and jumping around me. "Wanna go for a car ride, boy?" I asked him, walking toward the car. He knew what that meant. Gleefully, he ran over to the car and jumped excitedly around the door. I opened the door and he bolted into the back seat. I put the collar on him, saving the leash for when we got there.

Then I went back in to get my purse and the two kitties, who were still chorusing in disapproval of their recent change of venue. As I picked them up, little paws came out of the holes, desperate to be free. "I know, guys. I'm sorry. It will be over soon." I placed them in the front seat with me. Willie, smelling his two buddies in the car, began to bark excitedly. "Stop it, Willie. Cut it out," I admonished him. He paced back and forth across the backseat while the cats continued their growls and mews. Gosh, this is fun, I thought as I started the car.

It was a short ride to the vet's office—just a couple of miles. As I pulled into the driveway, Willie came to full attention. He spotted a beagle in a nearby car who was barking wildly and ricocheting from the back to the front seat. Willie began to bark at the sight of his new friend. Oh, boy, I thought. As I stepped out of the car, Willie launched himself from the backseat to the front, nearly knocking over the two cat carriers. I decided to take the cats in first, then come back for Willie. I went to the passenger-side door, opened it, and was nearly mowed over by Willie, who by this time had worked himself into a frenzy of barking and clearly wanted to go meet his new pal. Several other dogs in nearby cars had also started barking.

Naturally, Willie tried to jump out the door, stepping heavily on the cat carriers. I grabbed the leash and latched it onto his collar. The cats were also squawking now, sensing Willie's excitement. I took Willie around the car and put him in the very back, behind the second seat. Completely foolish, I realized, because by the time I got to the front door to get the cats, he had leaped over both seats. It was like Groundhog Day all over again. What was I thinking? I finally decided to just take Willie in and come back for the cats while the doctor examined him.

Willie bounded out the car door. The choker collar started to do its job as we approached the vet's office. Willie seemed to have super-human (or should I say, *supercanine*) strength. I held him in check, my arm nearly breaking. I was clearly not the alpha dog at that moment. I gripped the collar. Willie strained against it, choking and gasping all the while. That was how we entered the waiting room. If I thought my troubles were over then, I was sadly mistaken. As I stepped into the waiting room, I saw a bevy of animals: parakeets chirping, cats mewing, dogs barking. Willie was overcome with excitement. He continued to choke and gasp as I announced who we were. (I wanted to give a fake name at that moment.) I steered him to a nearby bench, pulled him close to my side on a short leash, and began to pet his head in an effort to calm him down. Willie did what any animal that suddenly realized they were at the vet would do: He started to shed hair. He shed enough hair in the next two minutes to knit an adult sweater. And he shook all over. People in the waiting room smiled knowingly at me as they held tightly to their own animals. It was obvious who was in charge in *my* situation. Thankfully, the technician came out shortly after that and took Willie to be weighed.

I ran to the car and brought in the two mewing kitties. By this time, I was sweating profusely, and I was worn out. An older gentleman who had witnessed the entire scene smiled at me and said, "Cats are a lot easier, aren't they?" I smiled in return, but I wanted to crawl in a nearby hole. I picked up the carriers and joined the doctor in the exam room. Willie was still shaking and shedding hair, but he had calmed down. "His paw's infected," the vet said. "We'll bandage it up, but he'll try to lick it. He'll need to wear a cone until it heals." He placed the cylinder around Willie's head. He swiveled and balked like someone had enclosed his head in a trunk. I held tightly onto his leash while the doctor examined the cats and gave them their shots. He helped me get them back in their carriers, and, like them, I just wanted to go home.

Twenty minutes later, we trooped out to a now full waiting room. Willie wound his way around my legs, the cone banging into them each time he turned. The technician brought out the cat carriers, smiled, and said, "Good luck." (Where had I heard that before?) Willie continued to gasp with his choker collar as I dug into my purse for my credit card—no small feat while holding onto my Cone Dog. I managed to get the card to the receptionist, and suddenly the room got quiet.

No barking, mewing, chirping animals. The same older gentleman looked at me and said, "I think yer dog just yerped."

"What?" I looked down, and there it was in living color: Willie's previous meal on display all over the inside of the cone. But it was not only in the cone; it had spilled from there to the surrounding floor. I was about to step in it. "Oh, no!" I gasped. One of the receptionists handed me a roll of paper towels. I tried not to gag as I cleaned up Willie's excitement. The waiting room people all turned away—trying not to gag themselves.

I don't even remember how I got the cats and Willie back into the car. All I remember is driving home. Willie, in true doggie fashion, jumped from the backseat into the front and cozied up next to me as if to say he was sorry for all the trouble. I would have forgiven him then, but every time he turned to look at me, his cone bopped me in the head. I was covered in doggie hair and even a few stray cat hairs as we pulled into the driveway. When I opened the door, Willie jumped over me, cone, leash, and all. I let him go. My first order of business was to call up that alpha male. I had a job for him in the near future.

Hind-Sight

I first saw Bo in the front yard of the new dental office in the town where I grew up. I had chipped a tooth eating something I shouldn't have while visiting my parents, and they had encouraged me to try the new dentist. He had just opened his practice and wouldn't be that busy, they prodded. Why not? I thought. It would be convenient. When I pulled up to the office, a dog was sitting on the front lawn. I got out of the car and the dog greeted me immediately. Wagging its tail in the friendliest of ways, it came over to me and gave me the initial sniff test. I reached down to pat this friendly animal. It was a lovely mix of browns and golds, longish hair, and the biggest brown eyes I had ever seen in a dog. Something caught my eye then, and I looked up to see a tall, blond, muscular gentleman standing in the doorway. I was thunderstruck. I kept patting the dog, who was definitely continuing the sniff test, and stared at the person in the doorway.

The man smiled and opened the door. "Are you my three o'clock?" he queried, still smiling. I nodded in the dumbest, most inane way possible. I was mute. Who was this gorgeous guy? Why hadn't I known he was in town? "C'mon, Bo, c'mon girl," he called to the dog, who obeyed him instantly, wagging her tail the whole time. She jumped inside the dental office and lay down in the waiting room. I walked toward the door feeling like I had moon boots on. What the heck was wrong with me? The man kept smiling. "C'mon into the operatory," he suggested, pointing to a room to the right of the waiting room.

I nodded and stepped into a sparkling-clean room, complete with dental chair and a woman who was standing near the chair, also smiling at me. She asked me to sit in the chair. I realized then that I still had my sweater coat on. I knew I had to remove it, but the problem was, I was clutching my car keys in my hand. It seemed I had lost any brain cells I had left. I struggled to remove the sweater coat. Amused at my obvious attraction to him, the dentist came over and helped me get the coat off. He hung it up on a hook in the hallway just outside the room.

By this time, my face was deep crimson. Intellectually, I knew the way I was acting was ridiculous. Emotionally, I couldn't move, speak, or think. And I was still clutching my car keys. What to do, what to do, I thought. As I gazed around the room like I had all the time in the world before sitting in the dental chair, I spied a kind of half-wall partition at the left side of the room. With a graceful *schwing*, I casually threw my keys, so they would land on top of the partition. Time slowed measurably; I felt like I was in a kind of time warp as I followed the trajectory of the keys. They sailed up and over the top of the partition, knocking off an array of tools secured to a magnetic strip behind the wall, and landed on the floor behind it, clinking loudly.

The dentist and his assistant gazed at me and then at the partition. I was jolted back to reality. What did I do next? Why, I got down on my hands and knees and crawled over to the partition and behind it, my hind end in full display. (This was not my most outstanding feature...)

The dentist, who by now must have thought I was completely insane, came over. "You know, I know my way around here, why not let me get those for you?"

I was so embarrassed by my behavior that I wanted to stay right there on the floor. I realized then that my rear end needed to be lowered. I scrambled up, muttered something like "Thanks," and dutifully retreated to the chair.

Somehow, we got through the rest of the appointment. When I left the office, I vowed I would never see that dentist again. How humiliating! I just wanted to run away. As I left, Bo greeted me again, licking my hand as I left as if to say, *Yes, go lick your wounds. Goodbye and good luck.*

• • •

As it turned out, I *would* see that dentist again. Yesiree, right in the middle of the local grocery store. I was returning from a trip to New York to visit a guy I had been dating, who turned out to be a complete jerk. I was headed home two days earlier than expected and had decided to spend some time with my parents to recover from the hurt and disappointment. My father had picked me up at the airport, and on the way home, we stopped at the grocery store. I ran in, picked up a few groceries, and headed to the checkout. And there he was.

He was wearing a plaid flannel shirt and jeans. He was checking out, too, at the counter across from me. "So, back early from your trip?" he said.

I nearly fell over. "How did you know that?" I asked incredulously.

"Oh, your grandmother came into the office the other day. She told me all about it," he finished, flashing that smile that made me weak in the knees.

"Yeah, the guy was a real jerk," I explained.

"So," he continued, "what are you doing tonight?"

At this point, everyone at the checkout counter, including nearby staff who were stocking shelves, stopped. They all froze, waiting for my answer. After all, this was the new dentist in town, and I had grown up here.

When I arrived home, I skipped out of the car, where my mother waited with outstretched arms to comfort me after my horrific weekend. She was shocked when I hugged her hard and said, "I have a date tonight!"

This was the first of many dates with the dentist. While I was deliriously happy, one player in the scenario was not. That was Bo, the sweet brown-eyed dog that had greeted me so warmly that first day at the dental office. The problem was that she was no longer the first girl anymore. I had taken her place. Bo was nice to me but drew the line when it came to a ride in the dentist's truck. She quickly established the boundary: She jumped into the old red Chevy and parked herself right next to her master. Cajoling, offering treats, even trying to slide her over so *I* could sit next to the dentist, didn't work. There are some battles you fight, but this wasn't one of them. After all, I had suddenly taken a lot of attention away from this loyal dog. As time went on, Bo became very special to me. She really did have a sweet disposition. She had accepted the fact that I wasn't going away, although she always played the wild card when we got in the truck.

A few years later, it was very distressing to see Bo in obvious discomfort. She kept scratching and scratching her hindquarters to the point of rawness. We knew it couldn't be fleas; we had been faithful about giving her the monthly medicine. We didn't know what was going on. It was time for a trip to the vet. Since it was summer, I had time off, so I was the logical one to take her to the vet. We knew the vet well; his name was George, and he had a superb sense of humor. (Who wouldn't, after putting your arm halfway up a cow's rear end to examine it?) He was also a superior vet, and we trusted him completely.

The day of the appointment, we arrived to find a full waiting room. (Isn't that always the way?) Bo smelled those unmistakable smells that inform all dogs that this was not going to be a fun visit. She was docile and compliant, though, as I brought her into the waiting area. The receptionist, who also doubled as a vet tech, greeted me warmly.

"So, what's the problem with Bo today?' she asked. All heads turned in curiosity.

"Well, she won't stop itching and scratching her hindquarters," I offered.

"Well, let's have a look," the vet tech said, motioning for me to bring her up to the desk. In the most indelicate manner, she lifted up Bo's tail, took one look, and pronounced, "Yep. Anal sex."

I nearly gasped out loud. "What??"

The vet tech smiled at me with confidence. "It's clear to me it's anal sex."

I had a flashback to a time when I was a kid. Our dog, Ginger, had been "caught" by a neighborhood dog. They looked like they were stuck together—but I found out later what was really going on under Ginger's tail.

"No, not my dog," I told her firmly.

At this point everyone had stopped talking. All eyes were on me and the vet tech.

"Excuse me?" she said, looking confused. "It is without a doubt anal sex. Just look at the seepage," she finished.

I looked at Bo. I could feel my face getting redder.

"No—she's fixed; it couldn't be," I shot back, determined to let her know my dog had not engaged in such an activity.

"Fixed? Well, yes, but still this can happen," she said in a reassuring voice.

"My dog has not done that," I said, knowing I was being *tres* defensive and speaking louder than I needed to.

You could hear a pin drop in the room. The tension was obvious. Not even a squeak from the parrot in the cage hanging from the ceiling.

"Done what? Oh, my God—anal *sacs*, s-a-c-s," she spelled out, laughing uproariously. "The anal *sacs* in her hindquarters are infected. Oh, my God, you thought—holy cow! Wait till I tell George!"

The entire waiting room erupted into laughter. I was relieved but oh, *so* embarrassed.

A few minutes later, we were called to have George check Bo out. The vet tech called out as we trooped down the hall, "Oh, George, the anal sex dog is on her way…"

The fun part of this visit was explaining the misunderstanding to my husband—yes, my husband, the dentist. I did end up marrying him. It seems that Bo and I had both shared an interesting moment of "hind-sight."

Deirdre, the Dog-Walker

Leaving the small coastal town where I grew up was heartbreaking. The shelter and familiarity of a place that had given me a solid sense of myself was about to be abandoned. Abandoned for a more cosmopolitan city with its big population, big-city noises, big schools. My own old high school had become crippled in its inadequacy; it could not keep up with the times and eventually lost its accreditation—just when my son, Ben, was about to enter high school. The decision to relocate where there were better schools was doubly difficult because I was a teacher in one of my hometown's elementary schools. Loren's dental practice had thrived there; the townspeople had been good to him. Our kids loved the neighborhood they were in—they walked to school every day and never had a shortage of kids to connect with. It was idyllic until the downfall of the school system.

Once we decided to leave, though, it didn't take us long to find a beautiful little cabin on a lake just outside of the city where my kids would go to school and where I would hopefully find another teaching job. The road leading to the cabin was a rough dirt road with potholes and bumpy rocks along the way. It wound down and down like a spiral staircase until it flattened out at the edge of the lake. We didn't seem to mind the road at the time. The surroundings were breathtaking: rolling hills everywhere and the added bonus of a winding creek that spilled into the lake on our property. Woods surrounded us on all sides and provided privacy near the shoreline. We were in love with the place even as our hearts ached with nostalgia at what we were leaving behind.

There were few year-round residents on the road at the time, probably because of the challenge it presented in the winter. There were four or five small quaint cabins before our home and several more just beyond the creek. All these were occupied in summertime only. We learned from the realtor that the people on the road were very "nice and friendly"—although most were retired, she had added.

We moved that summer, and as we settled in over the next several weeks, unpacking box after box, we began to notice a parade of sorts on the road in front of the house. It progressed from cars slowing down as their occupants peered at the house, to people walking by and stopping to talk with each other in front of the house, to two people actually stopping in with brownies to welcome us to the neighborhood. We laughed about everyone's obvious curiosity about us and quickly realized that the people on the road had all lived there for many years. In the cast of curious characters who seemed to pass by our house each day, one stood out. She was an elderly woman, or so she appeared because of her obvious difficulties in walking. She was slightly bent and very heavy-set, moved very slowly, and never looked at the house when she passed by. This struck me as quite a paradox compared to the rest of the inquisitive neighbors.

She wasn't alone, though: She had two dogs with her who explored every inch of the road on their morning trek. She would call loudly to them to come back when they strayed into nearby yards and left their mark on plants and bushes. One of the dogs moved as slowly as she did. He was an old basset hound whose stomach nearly dragged on the ground as he took one laborious step after another. The second dog was a hyper mix of beagle and springer. He catapulted into yards at lightning speed, jumped over boulders or other objects in his path, and didn't heed the call to come back to his owner. I began to watch for this same scene every morning as I drank my coffee and looked out the window. As the summer progressed, so did the scene with the old woman and her two dogs. She now carried a fly swatter with her and wore an old fishing hat pulled down around her ears. She fanned and flailed her fly swatter in a way that was reminiscent of an Egyptian slave cooling an ancient pharaoh. The hyper dog would come to the edge of our yard, sniff the ground, and immediately leave his mark. He didn't wander too close to the house—probably because we had a dog of our own.

Willie, our chocolate lab/golden retriever mix, was a big dog with thick, wavy golden hair. He had been displaced by the move and barked at everything that went by the house that summer including trucks, cars, squirrels—and particularly people. He always knew when the old woman and her dogs went by even when he was inside the house, and he would bark ferociously to let them know they were on his turf. (We also had the two cats, of course, and they loved their new woodsy surroundings. They were great hunters, and the squirrel, chipmunk, and bird populations were greatly reduced after their arrival in the neighborhood.)

The morning pattern continued with the old woman for the rest of that summer. I learned from the realtor, who checked in to see how we were faring, that her name was Deirdre. She was a long-time summer resident and stayed each year until the air turned chilly in October. She had medical problems, and her doctor had recommended she walk each day to alleviate them. She loved animals, especially dogs, and was active in the local animal shelter. All this information endeared me to Deirdre, the quirky old lady who walked by my house each morning.

That fall when school started up, my kids and I all began our new adventures in the "big-city" schools. I had been hired to teach in the middle school and was pretty apprehensive about it. The school was huge compared to the tiny K-5 school I had taught in before, and I was teaching sixth grade—a grade I had never taught before. The first day, I had the jitters, and as I tore out of my yard and headed down the dirt road, I nearly ran over Deirdre and her dogs. She was walking squarely in the middle of the road. Couldn't she hear my car coming? I slowed down as she lumbered to the side, gathering up her dogs. I smiled as I passed her, but was met with an icy, cold stare. I immediately felt guilty at speeding out of my driveway and drove slowly the rest of the way up the winding dirt hill.

I casually mentioned this incident to Loren that night at dinner. (He had left much earlier than me to commute to his practice in the small town we had moved from.) He just smiled and teased me about being a madwoman on the road.

The next morning, as I crept out of my driveway, I noticed a small but boldly painted sign nailed to a tree alongside the road. It read: **15 miles an hour**. I laughed out loud at the obvious message to me—hmm; who had put that sign up? Sure enough, Deirdre was walking in the middle of the road as I rounded the corner to head up the hill. Once again, I slowed to a crawl as she pulled her dogs to safety at the side of the road. I smiled and waved but got the same icy stare in response. Really? This was a little ridiculous. I wasn't going *that* fast; I knew it wasn't 15 miles an hour, but come on.

When I returned home that afternoon, I was shocked to see that **15 miles an hour** signs had been put up all along the road! Good grief! I felt like a two-year-old being reprimanded! My husband laughed when I came storming into the house. Who was this Deirdre, anyway? The road was managed by an informal road association; it was not a public road monitored by the local police. My kindly feelings toward Deirdre the Dog-Lover were quickly fading. Each morning, I would meet Deirdre on the road. I made a conscious effort to go slow but did forget some mornings, only to feel total regret when I received her admonishing stare. I was relieved when the weather turned colder, as I knew Deirdre would be heading back to Massachusetts. Now I could go 25 miles an hour up and down the road to my heart's content!

We survived the winter in our new house even with the challenges of the snowy, icy road, and the next summer began in much the same way as the first one—neighbors walking by every day, Deirdre included. Only now, her hyper dog ventured farther into the yard. Every morning, like clockwork, the dog would scamper around on the deck that encircled most of the house. It sounded like a herd of buffaloes. Willie would go crazy, tearing around the inside of the house from window to window in a barking frenzy. This, in turn, fueled Deirdre's dog, who sometimes, did it again just for good measure. But Deirdre was nowhere to be seen when this happened.

One day, I decided to get up early and see what was going on. Sure enough, Deirdre toddled up the road in front of our house accompanied by her two dogs. The hyper dog bolted from her side and ran into our yard. Deirdre gave a feeble call to him but kept right on walking. I couldn't believe it! The next morning, I got up early again to prepare for the dog's deck run, though I wasn't sure what I was going to do. As I rinsed out a coffee cup at the sink, I heard the thunder of the dog's feet as he rounded the deck. This time, though, he had a purpose: He was chasing my tiger cat, Jazz. Jazz looked terrified but made a leap onto the side of the gazebo next to the deck and scratched his way to the top of the roof. Willie went crazy barking as I watched the hyper dog stand on his haunches and bark at the cat. All of a sudden, I heard Deirdre's voice. "Come on, now, Eddie. Get down. C'mon, let's go home before you wake someone up."

Before I knew what had happened, I heard myself say, "Too late. I'm awake now."

The effect was immediate. Deirdre, startled by my voice, turned toward me at the window. "Sorry—Eddie loves to chase cats."

"He runs around our deck every morning. Willie goes crazy."

"Oh, that's your dog's name. I've seen him in the yard. He's a sweetie."

Sweetie was not in my vocabulary at the moment. I was thinking about **15 miles an hour**. We stared at each other for a few moments. Then Deirdre grabbed Eddie's collar and pulled him back toward the road. With no resolution in sight, I was left with feelings of frustration and annoyance.

The next morning, there was no sign of Eddie...nor the morning after that. I began to relax and develop a feeling of smugness that I had won the Battle of the Dog-Walker. I let Willie out as soon as I got up each morning. There was no sign of Deirdre anywhere. Had something happened to her? Then one morning after I had let Willie out, something caught my eye outside my upstairs bedroom window. It was Deirdre, her two dogs, and Willie, all kibitzing like old friends by the edge of the property. I watched in astonishment as Deirdre took something out of her pocket and held it out for Willie. It had the familiar shape of a dog biscuit, and Willie gobbled it up like there was no tomorrow. My own dog had given up his loyalty to his family, all for a treat! Deirdre 's other two dogs waited expectantly for their treats, as well. So *that's* why Eddie no longer thundered around on our deck! Clever old lady, I thought.

When school started again that fall, I purposely looked for Deirdre each morning. But she wasn't there. When I mentioned this to Loren, he said, "Oh, she walks earlier now. I pass her every morning on my way to work. She's always in the middle of the road." Slightly relieved, I went about my life, no longer worrying about Deirdre and her dogs. Several new houses went up around the corner from us—more new neighbors, some with kids in high school. By the time summer came again, there was a lot more traffic on the road.

As I came home from grocery shopping one day, I noticed a new handwritten sign stuck into the ground at the sharp corner to our lake road. It read: "Walkers on road. SLOW DOWN." I chortled out loud—that had to be Deirdre. She must have returned. I looked for her the next morning and there she was. But she was somehow different. There was more life to her movements. In fact, she looked like she had lost a lot of weight. All that walking was really paying off! I noticed she had only Eddie with her; the other dog was nowhere to be seen. Willie was overjoyed to see her, of course. I watched in amusement as she handed him a biscuit while Hyper Dog danced about her, barely able to wait his turn. She walked on, spritely now. I shook my head.

Later that summer, my family and I noticed a change in Willie. He was getting older; in fact, he was almost twelve. His face had turned white in contrast to his golden fur. He walked a little more slowly and seemed to sleep a lot. One hot, humid day we took him down to the lake for a swim, and he was like a little puppy. He swam circles around my husband in the lake, tromped through the grasses on shore trying to catch a bullfrog, and explored the nearby shoreline. We watched in amazement and pure joy his freedom and energy.

The next morning, though, Willie did not want to move. He didn't eat. He didn't drink water. My husband called to him, but he wouldn't get up. We finally coaxed him out into the yard to lie in the sun, and he stayed there for several hours. We called the vet. I went upstairs and cried quietly, fearing the worst. I worked in my gardens around the yard that afternoon, so I could keep an eye on Willie until we got him to the vet. A car pulled up by the driveway and stopped in the middle of the road. A young girl got out, and I recognized her as Deirdre's granddaughter, who frequently visited her in the summer. She was holding something in her hand. A dog biscuit. She was calling to Willie. Willie did not lift his head. I felt my eyes stinging as I stepped forward.

"Oh, I'm sorry. Willie is not feeling well today. He's hardly moved all morning. We're worried about him."

"What? What's wrong with Willie?" Deirdre stepped out of the car and hurried over to him. "Oh, no, what's wrong? Tell me what happened!" As she spoke, she bent down to gently pat Willie's head. He raised his head slightly and thumped his tail in recognition.

"I don't know what's wrong. We've called the vet. He won't eat or drink. He hardly moves." I could feel my eyes start to fill.

Deirdre looked up at me. "Now don't get me started," she said, as I noticed her eyes were as full as mine. "You know I lost my dog last year. Fourteen years old. I had to put him down. It nearly killed me," she said wiping her eyes with her hand. "Not Willie," she said. "He is the sweetest dog I've known. C'mon, Willie, you can get through this. That's a good boy." She knelt and rubbed his back. The granddaughter did the same. I watched as the two of them clucked over my dog. Then Deirdre stood up just as suddenly. "I'll keep my fingers crossed," she said, holding up her fingers to show me she meant it.

"Thank you," I mumbled, "thank you so much. And thank you for all the treats you've given him."

She paused for a moment and looked at me, then smiled and got back in her car—parked squarely in the middle of the road. My eyes filled again, but this time it had nothing to do with walkers on the road or a 15-mile-an-hour sign. It had everything to do with an old woman who had shown me her love of dogs.

Double Take

My best friend, Julie, lived down the street from me, just a quick walk past two other houses. She and I were both stay-at-home moms. It was a lonely occupation. Very few mothers stayed at home, at least not in our neck of the woods, and if they did, they were usually a lot younger. Julie and I hit it off right away. Our link was Julie's husband; I had gone to high school with him. Our kids were almost the same ages. We had a lot in common. Julie ran a day care and I ran a nursery school. We shared ideas about crafts, recipes, and above all, hummingbirds and flowers. We especially talked about flowers. Julie had a natural knack for growing them. I envied her ability to grow the most magnificent clematis, for example. Every year, the blossoms multiplied, yielding a most gorgeous display of purple and pink that hung heavily from the trellis in her front yard. I particularly envied her flock (and I do mean *flock*) of hummingbirds that zoomed in and out of her backyard—so much so that I went out and bought eight fuchsia plants to hang on my porch. Reportedly, these plants were hummingbird magnets. Julie just laughed at me and said, "You'll go to any lengths to steal my hummingbirds, won't you?" The humming-birds *did* show up. If only I had watered my fuchsias more frequently, they might have visited more often…

One day, Julie and I were sitting in her kitchen, gabbing away. The four kids were playing together—or should I say, Jessie, Julie's daughter, and my son, Ben, were busy bickering. Justin, Julie's son,

117

and my daughter, Katy, were having a good time all on their own and trying to stay clear of the two bickering kids. Julie's dog, a beautiful mix that looked like a large fox, came into the kitchen as we were talking. Julie called to Justin, "Put Katy outside to go to the bathroom."

At that, Ben stopped his rant and looked directly at Julie. He was about eight years old at the time. "Katy doesn't need to go outside to the bathroom, Julie," he said pointedly.

Julie looked at me, puzzled. "Yes, she does, Ben. She's been inside now for several hours. It's time for her to go out. Put her out the back door, Justin."

Ben stood up to his full, skinny height and squared up with Julie. "Julie, Katy goes to the bathroom inside, like everybody." With that, he reached down and grabbed his sister's hand protectively.

"No, Ben—oh, my God! You thought I meant your *sister* Katy. No, no, I meant our *dog* Katy. Geez. I would never make your sister go outside to the bathroom."

We all started laughing. Ben, clearly relieved that his sister was going to be treated humanely, stepped away from Julie. He turned back to Jessie, ready to continue the argument, which he clearly enjoyed. Julie and I continued our talks over coffee. But every once in a while, Ben would peek into the kitchen, keeping a watchful eye on our neighbor.

Face of Crimson

Just Warming Up

Have you ever been to St. Andrews-by-the-Sea? It is a lovely coastal town over the border of Maine in New Brunswick, Canada. I had seen it written up in a number of magazines and also online as a great romantic getaway. I convinced my husband one fall weekend that it would be the perfect escape. Our kids were grown and out of the house. We had settled into a comfortable routine. It was time to shake things up a little. After driving for several hours, we arrived at this quaint little town. Visually, it lived up to its name. The buildings were charming and beautifully landscaped. There were lots of little shops lining the famous Water Street, beckoning visitors to explore them. I was excited to visit the Kingsbrae Gardens, too—they were supposed to be breathtaking.

Loren had surprised me by getting us a room at a beautiful inn right in the center of town. Our room was gorgeous—king-size four-poster bed, scented rose arrangements on the nightstands, lovely pictures in gilded frames on the wall. It spoke of a time from yesteryear. It was all terribly romantic. I kissed my husband sweetly as we left for dinner at a nearby restaurant. I had a few surprises of my own in store for this wonderful, considerate man.

When we returned to our room, full of good food and fine wine, we were both feeling quite amorous. I put on my slinky lingerie and sidled over to the bed, where Loren lay in anticipation. From my cosmetic bag on the nightstand, I pulled out a tube of "warming gel."

I had seen it advertised on TV many times. It was all discreetly done, of course, for prime-time television viewing, but the happy ending was clearly shown through a succession of fireworks displays. After the colorful display, the camera panned back to the happy couple who lay, complete with disheveled hair and smiles, on their bed. OK, so advertising really works, but I thought, What the heck! Let's spice up our love life. It took everything I had to actually buy the product. I was just praying that no one I knew would be in the drugstore at the same time. But here it was—the promise of fireworks. Loren smiled wickedly when he saw the tube in my hand.

It did not take long—maybe ten seconds after I applied the gel—to realize the fireworks were already starting. But not the kind you would hope for. It felt like my entire nether region would burst into flames. It was so hot I wanted to scream, and in fact, I did. Loren was alarmed and understood what was happening by the expression on my face.

"Oh, my God!" I yelled. "I'm on fire!" I bolted off the bed, ran into the bathroom, and grabbed an icy-cold washcloth. I gently tried to wipe off the gel, but to no avail. It had seeped into the very pores of the Mound of Venus—minus the love. "Hot Lips" had a new meaning. I kept yelling, "Oh, my God! Oo-o-o—it's burning!"

My thoughtful husband came in and started a tepid bath in the beautiful Victorian tub with gilded feet. I didn't notice. My mission was to get in and get relief. The tub helped somewhat, but the damage was done. So was the night of getaway romance. I finally fell asleep sometime in the wee hours of the morning with a cold, wet facecloth thrown over my burning parts.

The next morning, we dressed and got ready to head for home. When we came downstairs, I noticed a number of people were staring at us and smiling. I realized the walls must have been very thin and they had heard me yelling...

Unfortunately, the burn didn't go away, and I knew I had reacted allergically to the gel. We needed to get home, and I needed to get to the doctor.

I got an appointment the next day. When I explained to the nurse what had happened, she stifled a smile. "That must have hurt," she said, barely concealing her amusement.

When the doctor came in to examine me, I told my story one more time. He looked up from his laptop. "Warming gel???" he said, as if he had not considered this option in his own life.

"Yes," I replied, "but I would recommend other ways to enjoy the fireworks."

Shake It, Baby!

It was my first year in a big city school after teaching at the elementary level for fifteen years, every grade except second. Those schools had been rural—small-town populations, close-knit communities, and multilayered responsibilities throughout the school day. Now I was faced with an entirely new environment. The city school itself was gargantuan compared to what I had taught in. It had two stories, with the sixth-grade classrooms all in one wing. Now instead of a K-5 school with one class per grade, there were six sixth grades. The school seemed like a giant maze to me, but it was beautiful. The art room and library were feasts for the eyes with their colors, their wall decorations, and plentiful books everywhere.

Leaving my hometown had been a very difficult move. My husband—"Doc Painless"—had a dental practice there. Our kids had to leave behind their friends and the comfortable neighborhood we'd lived in. All in all, moving closer to the "big city" was a culture shock for us as a family. My mother had died that summer, too, leaving a gaping hole in my heart. We had lots of adjusting to do.

Luckily, a former colleague of mine had also moved to the big city school. Years before, we had taught together in a small school outside the city, but she had been in this city school for a number of years. She helped me transition into the daily schedule, routines, and curriculum of my new position. It looked like I would be teaching all subjects in a self-contained classroom, and she warned me that my incoming class would be big. In fact, this year, all the sixth grades were going to have huge numbers—twenty-eight to be exact. I gulped—I had been used to sixteen to eighteen kids in a classroom. Not only that, she told me with a grave face, I would also have the "cream of the crop" kids. Normally, this is sweet music to a teacher's ears, but she went on to say that I would have a lot of pressure because this was such a gifted class. I had everyone from the well-known rabbi's daughter to the Spanish teacher's child, to a senator's son. I considered opting for a new career, but it was only a fleeting moment of panic.

I practiced upping my vocabulary that first wild week at the school. I had taught third grade for a number of years and quickly realized that in sixth grade that translated as "baby talk." The challenges continued: The school's computer access was phenomenal. There was a giant computer lab where every student could have access. At the time, this was not the case in most rural schools. I was familiar with computers but certainly lacked the skill base I realized I would need. There was also the class dynamics. I could barely move around the classroom, it was so filled with desks and bodies. Proximity to buddies led to discipline issues. And then, of course, this was a group of kids who thought they knew *everything*! I had to learn the content in all new subjects. Classes were held every day in every subject. I had to be really *on*. I was studying my curriculum material at night in an effort to stay ahead of the kids. And they did know a lot.

One of my students was the son of a then US Senator, and his mother was a teacher in the same school system. (No pressure there!) That year, the senator decided to run for governor and he won! There was a flurry of excitement in the school and in my classroom. There were lessons on gubernatorial races. And then there was the *invitation*. Following the inauguration of the governor, the entire class and I were invited to the governor's mansion, an hour and a half away, for a meet-and-greet "tea." Another teacher, who had the governor's son for an accelerated course, was also invited. We were so excited! Everyone was on their own for transportation, since the event was on a Saturday. The other teacher and I decided to ride together.

Of course, this was January in Maine. And of course, that is one of the snowiest, coldest months of the year. A day before the tea, there was a bad snowstorm. The interstate had been well-plowed, but there were still some icy spots. The other teacher and I left about two hours ahead of time, as we knew the drive would be slow going. The roads were awful. We were still excited, though. We were dressed to the hilt in warm woolen sweaters and heavy coats to combat the weather.

We arrived at the capital with only a few minutes to spare. We had been instructed to get to the governor's mansion by a certain time because they would then close the doors for security reasons. We knew there was only one solution: We had to run. And so, we did, high-heeled boots and all over the dicey, slick sidewalks. We started laughing because we must have looked ridiculous. When we arrived, I was sweating profusely—for a number of reasons. I had been running, sure, but I was also going through perimenopause. Hot flashes, sweating, and hormonal swings were part of my daily life now.

My colleague and I entered the first meet-and-greet venue, a tent that was, thankfully, heated with space heaters. And thank goodness we had made it! The kids from the class were bopping around the room, munching on the generous snacks that covered the many folding tables. They were happy to see us. I dabbed sweat off my face and smiled. We made our way to the table to get a snack. The governor was nowhere to be seen, and we learned from one of his officials that we would actually meet him in one of the mansion's stately rooms as Phase Two of the meet-and-greet. We munched on hors d'oeuvres. No one took our coats. There didn't seem to be anywhere to put them.

Soon there was a formal announcement to come into the governor's mansion, and we all filed in dutifully. My colleague and I had unbuttoned our coats by this time, but I continued to sweat and feel the flush of the hot flash that wouldn't go away on my face. My cheeks began to hurt from smiling so much. Soon the governor, his son, and his wife appeared. Everyone clapped. At that point, the governor gave a short speech about perseverance and other motivating factors, but honestly, I don't recall what he said. I was too busy sweating. I had on my fake-fur "bear coat" (as I liked to call it) and numerous warm layers under that. I wanted to tear everything off and run through the snow.

At that moment, however, drinks were served by the staff, and I was handed a cup of hot, steaming coffee in the daintiest, most beautiful cup ever. I glanced at my colleague, who could see what was going on. She smiled and stifled a giggle. She had already gone through menopause. I must have looked like I'd just stepped out of a sauna. I'm sure my mascara was running down my face, as I had wiped it so many times in an effort to wipe away the sweat rivulets. I drank the coffee. Our coats were still on. There was no offer to take them, probably because we had arrived late. I wanted to cry because my hormones were out of control anyway, I was nervous, and I thought I might pass out from heat exhaustion. Meanwhile, the hot coffee worked its magic. My sweating and flushing became worse. In retrospect, I wonder why I didn't just throw my coat over my arm, but I was juggling a coffee cup and a nervous stomach, and I couldn't think straight.

A few minutes later, Phase Three took place. It was announced that the governor would have a formal meet-and-greet in the next room. We would go into the room in single file and shake the son's hand, the wife's hand, and then the governor's hand before we departed. By this time, I was miserable. I could hardly speak, and I knew that my mascara was truly smeared. But I also knew my duty as a teacher of middle school children.

My colleague and I were ushered in first. The governor's son shyly stuck out his hand, looked at my face, and then quickly looked down. I didn't think much about this—I just wanted to go outside. Next was the governor's wife, who pulled me to her for a bear hug. The last thing I wanted was cuddling and warmth. I was nearly catatonic from sweat. I turned then toward the governor. He smiled pleasantly at me and offered his hand. I tried to smile, sweat pouring down my face. His hand was cool—in fact, it was downright cold. And it was instant relief for all my woes. At that point, there was an involuntary, primal reaction on my part. I let out what sounded like an orgasmic groan and muttered, "Oo-o-o, your hand feels so nice and cold." My eyes may have rolled back in my head.

In an instant, two men in dark suits appeared out of nowhere. Apparently, they were security, and no woman was going to purr like that to the *governor*. I was whisked out of the room where—you guessed it—they finally took my coat… Not much fuss was made over me, though. The two men checked my coat, looked at my flushed, sweaty face, and wished me a good day. I was more than happy to go. The cool, snowy day awaited me outside.

When One Door Closes...

We all do it. Some of us do it regularly, some of us do it under duress, and some of us do it as a means of prevention. I'm talking about visits to the doctor, of course. I am one of those people who fear, honor, respect, and abhor going to the doctor. After all, I grew up hearing medical horror stories that my dad seemed to revel in telling my siblings and me. His dad had been a general physician way back when doctors made house visits. My father would accompany his dad sometimes, and somehow from those childhood visits, he became an expert in all medical matters. We believed every word he said until we realized later in life that he was not a doctor himself and never would be. And so, every year in fear and prevention, I would march myself to the doctor's office to get every nook, cranny, and crevice I owned checked.

On one particular visit, I remember feeling more trepidation than usual. My regular doctor, whom I had gone to for years, was on sabbatical for a year (how dare he?). He had gone through a nasty divorce and needed a new perspective on life. The other doctor who worked with him had started the practice and had been there for years. He was from Great Britain and had a fascinating accent. It made you feel good just to hear your cholesterol and weight gain numbers said with a foreign twist. He filled in whenever my doctor was away, so I was familiar with him, but I still preferred the comfort and familiarity of my own doctor. This particular year, I was signed up for an annual physical including all the fun woman stuff.

And when I say *fun woman stuff,* you know what that means, especially if you are a woman. There is nothing more humbling than lying on a hygienic tissue sheet wearing a precarious Johnny that could tell all in one wrong move, with your feet hitched up to stirrups. (In my case, my feet are quite long, so my toes seemed to dangle over the tops—another way to feel pretty in the moment…) Not only that, but the breezes are blowing across your most vulnerable parts. Worst of all, my face always belies my feelings: It is the color of a ripe tomato. A sweet young nurse was trying to make me feel at home. I knew her, too—she had been the one I grabbed by the collar while in labor with my daughter. Today she was very cheerful, and I soon realized why.

When the doctor came in, a whole new look crossed her face. In fact, a whole new look crossed *his* face, as well. It was unmistakable: They were in love. I knew that the doctor was married, but the nurse was not his wife. The two started talking excitedly about this and that. Meanwhile, I was exposed and waiting. The doctor had performed many internals, delivered many babies, and had sewn up a nasty gash my son had incurred years earlier. I knew he was competent. Some people said he could smell your breath and know if you had appendicitis! He had a good reputation, although I was thinking this might soon be ruined with the cute little nurse.

He said hello to me in that airy British accent, then, "Just relax your knees." Really? Easier said than done, but I obeyed like a good patient. As he started the exam, he continued to talk animatedly to the sweet little nurse beside him. I wanted to remind them that I was still lying on the table, but I don't think they would have heard me. Suddenly, I had the profound realization that the exam was not going the way it should have. This was supposed to be a vaginal exam. I spoke up as the most uncomfortable feeling came over me: "Ah, excuse me, Doctor. I, uh…think—"

"What? Oh!" he said, as he realized what was happening. "Oh, sorry," he quipped in his lovely accent, "wrong door!"

I burst out laughing, but the next time, I would come back to my regular doctor even if he didn't have that lovely British accent.

One-Stop Shop

I've always thought of myself as a liberated woman. Equal rights in the form of a paycheck, household chores, errands, and general overall fair treatment toward women. So why, as a liberated woman, did I find it so hard to pick up personal items at the local drugstore? You know what I mean when I say *personal*. No, not deodorant. Everyone needs to smell good if they're going to survive in the workplace. Not toothpaste. Don't we all want a white, bright smile? Not aspirin. We all get headaches. I remember my mother telling the story of how she found out about her menstrual period. She woke up one morning, sure she was dying when she saw what looked like carnage on her bedsheets. Back then, people didn't talk as openly about bodily functions or sex. No, I wasn't after feminine napkins—though I used to stuff them under the crackers or laundry detergent on the conveyor belt at the checkout. But here I was in a drugstore, which should have been familiar territory, nervous as all get-out. I had worked weekends at the local pharmacy while in high school. It was actually one of the few pharmacies in the area that still boasted a soda fountain. My job description was the epitome of a multitasker: I had to whip up ice-cream floats, point out where the hemorrhoid cream was, suggest a good restaurant in the area, ring up the prescriptions, find postcards of the town for tourists... and oh, yes, I had to dispense condoms when the occasion arose, so to speak. This last chore might have been the source of my drugstore trauma. The druggist, a kind man who could only be described as a

Count Dracula clone, was the one who explained it all to me. I was only sixteen at the time, and I was mortified that I even had to have this discussion at all. The condoms were kept in the back in special drawers. There were various colors, sizes, and to my shock, *sensitivities* to choose from. I could feel my face turning fifty shades of red as the Count pointed all these out in a very matter-of-fact tone. "Now, dear," the Count counseled me, "let them tell you what they're looking for." With a nod of his head and a dose of his inhaler, he headed to his favorite spot in the back where his pharmacy was set up: his swivel chair.

This was my cue to get back out front and wait on customers. How was I supposed to do that with visions of condoms dancing in my head? I knew the Count's routine. The swivel chair usually meant business was slow in the store, and it was a perfect time for a nap. The trouble was, I usually was the one who had to go out back and wake him up. He would startle, regain his composure, and then laugh in a high-pitched voice that only enhanced his scary facade. He praised me liberally and paid me well for working in his drugstore, so I dismissed any thoughts that he might really be a vampire in disguise. He also trusted me completely to run his store.

One Saturday night, he and his wife were going to a special event, and he was leaving me in charge. I was pretty confident I could handle the responsibility. I had only been there for an hour when I saw the face of a freshman at my high school peering through the giant front window. I immediately felt nervous, as this kid got into trouble wherever he went. I knew I could call my parents, who lived a mile away, in an emergency, which was a little reassuring. Sure enough, the kid swaggered into the drugstore with a leering grin directed right at me.

"Can I help you?" I said in my most aloof, professional drugstore voice.

"Oh, boy, can you ever! I need some rubbers." He looked straight at me.

I was stunned. So, this was it. This was my big moment of truth.

"What color and size do you want?" I shot back at him, but I knew my face was a dead giveaway.

He stole a look outside the front store window. I didn't see anyone. What was he looking at?

"Oh, give me extra-large pink," he said.

"Okey-dokey," I said, way too cheerfully. By this time, my face felt like I had eaten ten red-hot chili peppers. I walked to the back, found the "extra-large" drawer. Where were the pink ones? Oh, God! Where were they?

"We're out of pink. Will blue do?" I managed to choke out, realizing I had just made the world's worst rhyme. Just let this end, I thought.

"Sure, sure, hurry up. I need 'em fast."

I was wishing for a cold bucket of ice to put my face in.

I tried to look nonchalant as I dropped the box of twelve extra-large blue condoms into a brown bag with lightning speed. I rang up the total on the register. The kid threw some bills at me and bolted out of the store. It was then I heard howls of laughter, and three heads appeared in the front window. One of them was my customer. They all hooted and howled, waved the condom bag around, and took off. So, it had been a bet or a dare. No wonder the kid hadn't asked for condoms with *sensitivity*...

Maybe it was that pivotal moment of embarrassment that stuck with me throughout my life. Buying everyday items in a drugstore was just fine, but super-personal ones like hemorrhoid cooling pads, antidiarrheals, and—God forbid—those vaginal creams for the occasional pesky female itching problems required the purchase of other items so it wasn't obvious to other customers what was really going on in your life. So here I was on this particular occasion looking for one of those anti-itch creams. I scanned my surroundings as I pondered my choices: 1-day, 7-day? How about a suppository to put an end to everything? I grabbed the 7-day tube and threw it in my carrier along with other senseless purchases. I made it to the cash register with only one person ahead of me. The cashier handled the lady in front of me and her purchase of two items just fine, but when I stepped up to the counter, he was clearly overwhelmed. I had at least ten items, and I realized he must be new. He started to ring the items up, placing each one on the counter next to the register. He glanced behind me, muttered, "Oh, no!" and continued entering the purchases. I turned to look behind me and saw a line of eight people. Where did they come from? I wondered. The clerk finally finished ringing up my purchases, announced the total, and began packing everything into a plastic bag. With a smile of relief, he handed me the bags; one down, eight to go.

I thanked him, turned to walk out of the store, and heard a voice behind me call out, "Oh, miss! Miss! Wait! You forgot your Monistat!" I didn't know what to do first. I turned, feeling that age-old creep of red sliding up my face. The man was actually *waving* the tube of anti-itch vaginal cream like a flag on the Fourth of July. And he was dead serious. He didn't want me to forget my last item—the one the cashier had failed to put in the plastic bag along with all my other senseless items. Should I just turn and go, saying, "Oh, you must be mistaken!" or should I walk up to him, scratching myself and nodding knowingly to the eight people who were now staring at me with smirks and smiles on their faces? The itching had turned to burning. I needed the cream. I walked up to him, smiling at the eight other customers—and grabbed the tube out of his hand. At least it was dark outside.

Since then, I've been able to go into a drugstore and buy almost anything. As I mentioned before, I even bought a tube of "warming gel" for my husband and me, although there were some other senseless items in the basket. I never did buy condoms, though. I guess I am just too sensitive a person…

Pause a Moment

Daylight

T here is nothing like a good fight to help you rediscover your couch. And so, the couch and I bonded one Friday night after my husband and I fought over something simple that I had undoubtedly magnified about two hundred times. Our kids were grown and out of the house—our big, beautiful house nestled in the woods and overlooking a lake. And everything was changing in our lives at a rapid pace. Words like *retirement, assets, savings*, and *downsizing* bombarded us even though we were not ready to think about them. Our busy lives at work barely gave us time to think, much less to connect to each other. And of course, there were physical signs of change. (I remember scoffing at the word *menopause* and now was a full-fledged participant.) Perhaps that hormonal state [or lack thereof] precipitated the fight; or maybe it was the pictures of our kids on the stairway walls, smiling at us and reminding us that we were truly grownups. Whatever it was, the angry and hurtful exchange of words brought me to the couch in our daylight basement.

Loren had disappeared to our bedroom upstairs (why didn't I think of that?), and I was alone with my thoughts whether I liked it or not. I spent a restless night as a contortionist on the recliner end of the couch, miserable with the fight, miserable with the speedy passages of life, and miserable that I had chosen the couch. I dozed on and off, watching a movie on pay-per-view in between fitful spurts of sleep. The dog lay beside me on the floor, siding with me and guarding me, his "treat dispenser." I gazed out the back door for the umpteenth time waiting for daybreak, and I finally saw a hint of light outside. I checked the TV clock and saw it was five a.m. I heard telltale footsteps upstairs—could my husband really be awake at this hour? A moment later, he was standing in front of me, looking as disheveled and weary as I did.

"Didn't sleep," was all he said. My husband is a man of few words, but what he does say speaks volumes.

I didn't reply, still hurt from the fight. He knelt down in front of me then and buried his head in my chest. My heart soared, and I melted. My hands encircled his head and held on tightly. "I didn't sleep either," I managed to mumble.

He pulled away then and stood up again, looking at me.

"Let's get in the hot tub," he said.

He took my hand and walked me toward the door. For once, I said nothing, just followed him outside. It was barely light. We shed our clothes and nearly *ran* over the cold brick patio—it was only forty degrees—but I *really* ran in case the neighbors might be out. OK, it was barely light, and the woods screened us from our neighbors, but you never knew… We got in the tub and sighed at the welcome warmth. There was a pink hue all around us now as daylight was making its way into our little forest. We still did not speak, but we became aware of our surroundings. There was a rushing roar on the bank to our left. We looked toward the sound and were mesmerized: The recent snow-melt had unleashed a Spring Beast in the creek below us, and a burst of water jumped out of the culvert. It bent and wound around mossy rocks and gnarled trees weary from the winter. It gathered momentum at the end of the creek in eddies of swirling, frothy water, and then was abruptly still as it became a part of the lake in front of us. It acted out its vengeance against winter over and over and performed for us endlessly as we watched.

I felt myself breathe in deeply; the earthy aroma was overpowering. I gazed at the trees around us and saw they were plumped with night's rain, giving them a rich, dark-green color. The smell of spruce and pine were heady—memories of Christmas flashed in my mind.

Daylight

Loren and I stared up into the trees and waited. Light presented itself now in golden hues around us as the sun made its way into our little cove by the creek. And then we saw it. Just a flicker of movement, but unmistakable. Dressed in its black-and-white suit, a tiny chickadee flew tentatively over us and perched on one of the many bird feeders we had set up over the years. Startled by invisible ghosts, it suddenly swooped away to a nearby tree and let out a cry of *hey-sweetie, hey-sweetie*. There was an immediate and sudden rustle, and as if by magic, the trees were filled with endless chickadees. Where did they all come from? They were military perfection, sneaking up on the enemy before the final attack on the feeders! We watched them for the next several minutes, amazed at their ability to land on the feeders as their swerving, swooping landing patterns appeared so precarious. Then, after a frenzy of eating, they disappeared into the camouflage of the trees, their cry changing to a *chick-a-dee-dee-dee*. There was a shadowy movement overhead in the trees. The wingspan suggested a large bird, but it was hidden by the treetop canopy. Was it the eagle we had seen recently hunting over the lake?

My husband slid over next to me and took my now very prune-y hand. "I love you," he said simply.

I loved him all over again in that instant. In his quiet way, he had shown me a new day dawning, a new beginning. Change was good.

Makin' the Move

Part 1: Packing

The summer after I retired from teaching, Loren and I made a big decision. We were going to sell our beautiful home and move back to our hometown an hour away. My husband's office was still there, and he had commuted an hour each way for at least fifteen years. I, on the other hand, had lucked out with a twenty-minute commute. The goal was to get out of all existing debt and selling the big house on the lake would definitely help us do that. The problem was, I was very attached to our lakeside home. We had built it after a horrific fire burned the original house on the same property. Building the new house had been healing after the fire, but it had had its pitfalls. The contractor seemed to disappear for weeks at a time; subcontractors were hit and miss showing up to work. We finally discovered that our contractor was not paying his subcontractors; he was busy building his own house—with our money. With some luck and a lawyer, we finally straightened out the mess.

The results were worth the wait. A big cathedral ceiling with giant windows overlooking the lake were part of our eye-opening living room. A stone fireplace with a woodstove insert extended from floor to ceiling in the living room as well. It was breathtaking. Archways welcomed guests into the dining room and open kitchen. In short, it was everything we could have wanted in a house. But it required a lot of time, money, and energy to maintain. Heating it in the winter was difficult with the high ceilings. We often lost power in severe snowstorms, so much so that we bought a portable generator. Yet I loved the place. I had decorated it in light blues and creams; it was warm and inviting. It was also a blast to decorate for a number of holidays. Year after year, we had a giant twelve-foot Christmas tree that sparkled with blue ornaments and funky white furry ornaments that reminded me of snow. And Halloween—it was the perfect place to hang ghosts and goblins or place mini lit-up haunted houses on the mantel.

I also had my very own office, which Loren had remodeled for me. It was upstairs over the garage. Everything in this office was an expression of me and of my teaching job at the time. Signs that read "Trust your crazy ideas" hung over the windows. Pictures and notes from students lined one wall as a reminder to me that I was in the right career. Bookshelves held all my dearest picture books from teaching elementary school. It was my sanctuary from the world. And now we were going to leave it all behind. Rationally, I knew it was just a house. There would be another house in our future. We would downsize to a newer, smaller house that we could manage more easily and live out our "golden years" in. Emotionally, however, I was balking. I had grown comfortable in my "palace." It was an expression of my artistic side and an outlet for my creativity. Could I replicate all that in the tiny apartment we were destined to move into? We were also heading back to the town where I had grown up, where I'd met my husband, where we'd had our kids. Could I really go back? Didn't people warn about that? Financially, it all made sense.

The process of putting our house on the lake up for sale was also difficult. Not just emotionally, but practically speaking. I suddenly had to keep three floors of this big house clean. I knew I was no domestic goddess, and now other people were going to come and inspect every inch of the place. My sister, a former Realtor, came to the house to give me the scoop on what we needed to do to get it ready to sell.

"All the personal pictures of your family on the wall have to go," she said matter-of-factly as I stared at her in horror. "Too personal," she added. "You want people to feel like they can move in and make it their own home."

As we went from room to room, she pointed at the clutter on my bureaus, in my closet, on my bathroom counter. "It's gotta go," she said brutally.

I knew she was right, but now I had to start to really clean up all my messes. My messes of comfort and familiarity. I finally accepted that it had to be done. I set to work and became an organizational demon. The basement got cleaned out, closets were scoured, and even years of my teaching materials were sorted, discarded, or given away. I had taken the plunge. It was cleansing.

The next step was to convince Loren that he needed to do the same. This could be compared to pulling a pebble out of a cement block—nearly impossible and a daunting task. His "domain" consisted of the garage and his office—both of which were packed to the gunnels with every memory from the past fifteen years. Since the garage was the first place that people would see as they entered the house, that became the priority. My husband had formulated a plan for all this: He would pack up the garage, label everything in boxes, and then take it to the garage in our hometown. This sounded promising, but there was a big problem: The garage in our hometown was already packed to bursting with his *parents'* belongings, his old Austin-Healey, his sailboat, his dad's tools, a ping-pong table, a beer-making kit—you get the picture. There wasn't any room for the stuff from our house to go to the other garage.

Loren solved this dilemma by renting a storage unit halfway between our lake house and the garage in our hometown. At this point, we had some of our best arguments. Words like *hoarder, divorce, giant dumpster, Goodwill,* and *Let it go!* echoed between us. But we persevered. We would go to the garage in our hometown and plug away for several hours, cleaning one bay at a time. It was tedious and heartbreaking to watch my husband poke through his father's old tools and the projects the kids had made in school. I stayed clear because so much of the stuff was his and busied myself by looking at the endless boxes that had accumulated in the closets of the upstairs apartment.

One day, as my husband worked through a section of the garage, I amused myself by making a list of what I saw on the walls, floors, and shelves. Later, I put it into a rhyme that fit with the song "Raindrops on Roses" from *The Sound of Music*. (Even if you haven't seen this classic, I think you can relate...) It went like this:

Fish nets and wires
Old wreaths and some skates
Stacks of old tires
And Grandma's chipped plates
Boxes and boxes of nails and old tools—
Who are the
Real purging old fools?

Chorus:
Oh, when you must move
What does it prove?
It only makes you sad
I simply remember to keep packing my things
Until I am nearly mad!

Woolen hats and some feathers
Desk lights and a broom
Sandpaper and paint cans
Where did we find room?
Frames of old pictures
And Tupperware, too—
Bird seed in the trash can is
Making me blue...

(Chorus)

Logs in the corner
For some future fire
Fertilizer and bells
On Mom's worn out old dryer
A stuffed Easter bunny

Nailed to the wall
One push of the ladder
And it will all fall…

(Chorus)

I was so pleased with my little ditty that I sang it to my husband
as he toiled away in the garage. He wasn't amused. I busied myself with
the broom (which had to be pried out from under a number of piles)
and swept up one of many dust piles on the floor.

The process of sorting, throwing out, and packing was hard
enough. Added to this was the fact that we had to be ready for showings
at a moment's notice. Modern technology, while wonderful, added to
our misery. We had downloaded an app on our phones that let us
know when a potential buyer wanted to see the house. We knew when
this was going to happen because the phone emitted a loud *PING!*
So did Facebook and any text messages we were receiving. I began to
obsess over the phone. I had become completely Pavlovian: Every time
a bell sounded, I grabbed my phone and frantically checked to see if
there was a showing. I couldn't stop checking it. My clever husband
did not download the app—he received notifications via e-mail. He let
me do the worrying and concentrated on his free cell games whenever
he had spare time. (It beat cleaning the garage…)

If we did have a showing, there was a frantic check of bathrooms,
rugs, and garbage. I had recently had eye surgery. My new lens replacement was a plague: I now saw every speck of dirt a mile away. I had
become a Cyborg Clean Queen. Once the house was spit-spot clean,
we would hustle into the car, hoist our aging dog into the backseat
(thank God we didn't have to show the car—the backseat was covered
in hair), and scoot out of town. Then there was the waiting. Were
the potential buyers interested? We would soon find out, thanks to
our trusty phone app. Suddenly, our "palace" had become the object
of scrutiny and criticism. The potential buyers rated our house and
property on a scale of 1 to 5. Things we did not even worry about
surfaced. For example, some people did not like the natural waterfront

we had; they wanted a beach and wanted the trees cut down. Or they liked the light fixtures, but the kitchen counter wasn't up to par. (It actually could be replaced.) Not one mention of the beautiful stone fireplace, the cathedral ceilings, or the lovely finished basement. My husband took it all in stride, but I took it personally. I worried I was turning into a "house-zilla": What was wrong with my house, anyway?

Part 2: The Closing

Inevitably, we sold the house that summer. Two pings later on the app with a repeat visit clinched the deal. Or so we thought. The water test that the home inspector had done (at a very last-minute date, we thought) was clearly marked "FAILED." There were bacteria in the water—*coliform*—which we immediately looked up on our phones. We had been ingesting fecal animal matter for some time in our water... The water company guy that showed up to do the water treatment on our well explained it in more depth as we tried not to gag just thinking about it. "Animals go to the bathroom in the stream, the stream runs downhill and into your well. These bacteria aren't harmful on their own to humans [Really???], but it could join with other bacteria to form potentially hazardous conditions. The chlorine bleach should do the trick."

Two giant gallons of bleach and a dozen bleach tablets were poured down our deep well. And then the fun really began. In between packing up the house, we had to flush our well out to run the bleach through the system. We had a list of ten instructions to follow very carefully. All faucets had to be turned on full blast to facilitate this bleaching process. That would have been fine, except that, after two hours of this, our water level dropped to nothing. Dry as a bone. I quickly turned off all faucets and started to cry. How were we going to continue to flush out our well? What if we had no water? The summer had been extremely hot and dry—not a good thing for any well. Loren calmed me down and called our water guy. (He told us he was really a scientist.) He advised us to let it sit overnight and then hook up *one* faucet outside at a rate of a gallon a minute. My husband went out back and fussed with the hose, dutifully following Water Guy's instructions. Of course, we went out to dinner. We had no water, paper plates had been packed up, and the fridge was almost empty. We dragged ourselves to our apartment an hour away after dinner. At least that place had water AND a bathroom.

After several days of running our one hose (and traveling back and forth from the apartment an hour away), we tested the water for traces of chlorine. For this, we dropped a tablet into a Styrofoam cup with a little tap water in it. If it turned pink, even faintly, chlorine was still in the water. For days, the cup still had traces of chlorine. When the Water Guy came back to check the progress, he shook his head. I was distraught. We had postponed the closing, much to the ire of the potential buyers, and I was ready to let them drink all the fecal matter they wanted at this point. They also wanted to move in *before* the closing, as they had sold their house and were in a hotel. Tensions were mounting, and all parties involved were stressed and impatient to be done with this process.

Finally, after days of flushing the system, the water tested clear. My husband was a bit shocked when I jumped up and down gleefully at the test results and said, "Wow! I feel like I just found out I *wasn't* pregnant." Water Guy was a bit surprised, too, and commented that he had never seen anyone react in that manner. The sample was then sent away to the lab to be sure the coliform was gone from the bleach treatment.

It wasn't.

We got the report the day before our newly scheduled closing. (No stress there.) The next step was an ultraviolet filtration system to the tune of $1800.00. We were so weary by then, we just said, "Do it." A week later our water test came back clear! The system had done the trick! We scheduled the final closing.

Closings are usually just a formality and a flurry of signatures. Ours, of course, was not. The tensions of the water issue for our beautiful property had taken its toll on the wife of the buyer. She blew into the conference room of the lawyer's office with an angry look on her face and ATTITUDE oozing from her pores. She sat in one of the chairs and threw her very dark, Gothic-like hair over her shoulder. Then she slid down in the chair like a disgruntled teenager, making sure to avoid all eye contact with us, which was difficult considering we sat directly across from her. Her husband, an army lieutenant, was much politer. He shook our hands and made small talk as we waited for the lawyer to show up.

Meanwhile, the buyer's Realtor showed up. He was young, handsome, and very nervous. We didn't really know why he was there until we saw the wife of the buyer suddenly turn all her attention to him. She smiled sweetly and made cute remarks to him as if they shared a secret. He squirmed and seemed very uncomfortable with her flirtations. The husband did not seem to notice what was going on. When his wife turned back to face us, she hissed several times about how they had been living in a hotel next to a guest who played the guitar all night. "We haven't been sleeping," she sneered at us, barely making eye contact. We ignored this and talked about the beautiful creek on the property and the float that was at the edge of the dock. "We had to send the kids to Florida," she added, looking right at me with heavily made-up eyes.

"Oh, you have kids? That's great! I was hoping a family would move into the place. How many?"

"Three," answered the husband. "Two teenage girls and a middle school–aged son."

"My girls hate winter," the Goth Queen continued, "and I can hardly get my boy off his phone."

At this point, my husband and I looked at each other knowingly. The house was beautiful, but the mile-long dirt road and the snowy winters—sometimes two or three *feet* of snow, plus the power outages— were challenging, even for hearty souls like us.

The buyer husband quickly chimed in. "I plan on getting all the construction done on the house before winter sets in. I'm leaving for Afghanistan for a year in December," he finished proudly.

I swallowed a chuckle and could not look at my own husband for fear I'd burst out laughing. The house would be up for sale again in a year.

Part 3: The Move

In spite of all the trials and tribulations of the move, we headed back to my hometown the third week in July. We had fortunately recognized that we were not up for moving the furniture from three floors in our sold house to the three bays of the garage (which, incidentally, *did* get scoured out) below our hometown apartment, so we hired a moving outfit to do the job.

It is a bittersweet feeling to see your whole life wrapped, boxed up, and labeled for its future destination. The day of our move, I gazed around at the echoing rooms in our beloved house. I suddenly started to cry hard as the movers scurried about loading up the two (yes, I said *two*) big trucks with our crazy possessions. Loren gently guided me through the maze of boxes to the back deck. We sat on the steps and I leaned on his shoulder and let every one of my heartaches out in loud sobs. He held me close and said it would all work out and we would love being back by the ocean. He suggested I head down to the apartment, so I wouldn't have to watch our past life loaded onto the trucks one box at a time. I agreed and poured myself into the car. It was the longest hour's drive I had ever made.

At the end of the day, my husband called me from his truck.

"It's done. It's all loaded on. I'm coming home. The movers will be down tomorrow to unload."

I breathed a sigh of relief, but it still hurt.

"Oh, guess what?" Loren said then. "I found at least six huge jars of coins in the upstairs closet."

"Oh, yeah, I remember. They were too heavy to lug down to the kitchen. What did you do with them?"

"I took them to the bank. I dumped them into shopping bags. It took me three trips to carry them in. You know how they have those sorting machines that count the coins for you? Funny thing is, people just stared at me in the bank—at least at first—then they wouldn't even look at me by the time I was done. That machine is so loud, it sounds like a bulldozer. There were so many coins, it started to burn out. The manager finally came over to check the machine—and me—out. We looked down into the hole where the coins go, and you wouldn't believe it. There was a screw, a nail, a paper clip, and a tiny picture of Ben. It was jammed. The manager got it straightened out—finally. You won't believe it! We had $836.25 in coins. See, I told you it was good to save them!"

I had a sudden vision of my husband in the bank. He was already looking pretty smudged and dirty from lugging boxes and furniture, and that had been in the morning. He had on the one pair of shorts that the zipper didn't work very well on... The shopping bags full of coins had probably been a clue to the patrons that he was homeless...

Well, he kinda was. At least temporarily. I started to laugh out loud. Everything was going to be all right. In fact, we could plan a pretty nice vacation for $836.25.

Flower Fairy

I think my fascination with flowers began when I was just a little kid living in Virginia. We lived off Route 5 at the end of a mile-long dirt road. The road started off with a wide expanse of soybean fields bordering both sides, narrowed through a thick section of woods, and finally wound its way down a curved path that hugged a long boxwood hedge leading to our house. The James River flowed quietly behind the house. Every day, the bus would drop me off at the end of the road. My job as a big first grader was to walk the mile dirt road home. Looking back on this, you might call that neglect, but the community was deemed safe, and the people along the road all seemed nice. They all knew me well because I often stopped at their houses to visit as I made my way home. Most were retired, some were unemployed, and some—well, I don't know to this day why they were home during work hours.

One of these people lived just past the soybean field on the left. I never knew the name of the old man who lived there; I just knew it as Daffodil Farm. The house was a dilapidated old ranch that stood under a shady grove of trees, but next to it was a fairyland—at least to me. In the spring, Daffodil Farm came alive with color and sweet scent. Busloads of children visited; tourists visited; even the locals came to see the magnificent sight. I saw it every day. It fed my imagination and lit me up with a fiery determination to have flowers like that in my yard one day. Cool green velvet mosses interspersed throughout the banks of rolling daffodils lent a magical quality to the place. I pretended I was the Flower Fairy—adding a sprinkle of color here and there and opening the buds with a touch of my "wand"—an old stick I had found by the roadside. And oh, the colors! Sunburst yellows, snowy whites, sunset oranges. The flowers were planted in large groups. But the addition of arching trellises, wooden bridges over banks, and elf-like gnomes everywhere offered a promise of wishes granted. I would wander through the daffodils, making up stories and scenarios and talking out loud as I acted out my fantasies. The owner of the farm, an old and rickety gentleman, would often peer out his window when the dog inside his house announced the "intruder," but he never gave me a hard time or tried to shoo me away. Instead he would wave to me and the curtains would close.

I also discovered lilacs at our house along the river. We had four majestic bushes in our front yard, and their scent was intoxicating. I started drawing and coloring them. When our old dog, Nicky, died one summer, we buried him under one of the lilac bushes. He loved to lie under them in the shade. The following winter, a single lilac bloomed where Nicky was buried. Was it the nutrients from an old dog's bones? Or was it a reminder of life even in the still of winter?

Regardless, it only fueled my fascination for flowers.

And then, of course, there were royal-purple violets that covered a whole section of our yard. I loved to wander through this carpet of purple. It was then I started to sketch the arch inspired by Daffodil Farm with a vine of purple violets intertwined throughout it. This sketch followed me throughout my life; it would pop up when I was doodling or writing poetry for school, or on greeting cards that I thought I could use for a business. When we finally moved from our lovely home on the river, we downsized to a smaller house, but the property was alive with color and scent. There was a giant dogwood tree with creamy white blossoms, and I often climbed that tree and just sat and looked at the flowers. Then there was the crepe myrtle tree with its big, spongy, pink flower clusters. I took it all in. I would often explore the woods and nearby houses in search of flowers, and my mother never seemed to mind or worry. I remember her taking frequent afternoon naps—that was my cue to set out and discover what was growing all around me.

The best discovery of all was a house just down the street from ours. It was a huge colonial mansion that didn't really fit in with the simpler one-story ranch houses that lined the street. The giant boxwood hedge that encircled it sent a definite message of "Keep Out, We Like Our Privacy," but I could smell roses as I walked by. The scent was wonderful and inviting, and I took that to mean I should explore a little more. Without even thinking, I squeezed through the hedge and followed the scent of the roses. Toward the back of the house was a row of cedar hedges, but I was immediately curious about the arch-shaped entrance that someone had carved out of the hedges. When I stepped inside, I nearly fainted. There were flowers everywhere. I didn't know the names of all of them, but it didn't matter. The color hit me like a thousand rainbows. The flowers were arranged in wide, manicured rows with three or four feet between them. And the rows seemed endless. One whole row was devoted to roses of all colors and styles. I walked up to these velvety bundles and touched them gently.

And just then, someone called out to me, "You there, what are y'all doin' in my garden?"

I nearly jumped three feet. I turned to see a very old woman standing there, peering at me. Her face was not friendly. I was sure she was about a hundred from all the wrinkles and the wild white hair that stuck out everywhere on her head. She had thick glasses, which she adjusted with a crooked finger.

"Well, did y'all hear me? Who are y'all, anyway? Where do you come from?"

I'm sure I looked frightened, but my love of her flowers allayed my fear. I quickly told her my name and where I lived. I told her I had smelled the roses and that I thought her garden was magical. At that she suddenly smiled. "All right, then, y'all can *look* at the flowers but don't touch or pick any, ya hear?"

She ambled back into her house and closed the door. I never

knew her name, but I did visit the garden often. Sometimes she would come out and weed a little, but it was obviously a painful task for her; other times I didn't see her at all.

Besides my love of flowers and related fantasies, I also loved to pretend I was a teacher. Being an only child for ten years forced me to amuse myself, which I did by dressing up my five dogs and making them sit at my little wooden table (very uncomfortably in wooden chairs) and pay attention while I taught them math or read aloud to them from one of my books. My flower destiny was eventually usurped by my teaching destiny, but I did not forget about my love of flowers. Gorgeous colors and scents found their way into the gardens I created around every home I lived in. Gardening became my hobby, and it was a great escape from the stresses of teaching. One day I looked around my closet as I was trying to decide what to wear, and I realized that most articles of clothing I owned had some kind of flower design on them! Even my jewelry had flower themes. I had spotted a gorgeous single-flower necklace while on vacation in Florida. There were shades of yellow in it that were reminiscent of Daffodil Farm…

• • •

When my brother got sick with kidney cancer, my life came into sharper focus. Yes, I loved teaching, but I had been at it for thirty-two years. What was I doing? What was my passion? What did I want to do for fun while I still could? I decided to retire several years earlier than most. People at school asked me, "What will you do? How will you fill your days after such a busy schedule?"

The answer was obvious: It was evident in the six gardens around my house, in the books and magazines about flowers that lay on my coffee table, and in the fact that I had signed up for floral design classes that fall. Even my retirement speech was a comparison of flowers to teaching: "So, go ahead, be a 'pistil.' Be bold, 'petal' ahead, plant your positive roots in your students, be a 'composite' of fun." So corny, but it was so ingrained in me. What was I waiting for? I could just picture a beautiful metal archway in front of my flower shop, dotted with purple velvet violets and yellow daffodils, welcoming people to come in to a new fairyland of imagination.

The Story

Storytelling has always been a big part of my family. I remember even as a little girl that when Great Uncle Buddy, Uncle Skip, Great-Aunt Katherine, Great-Aunt Gloria, and my Grandmother Bine (don't ask; we don't know either...) all got together, several things happened: The noise level increased ten decibels, laughing ensued, and The Story was told. The Story was always different each time the family gathered, and there was an endless supply of them: There were seven siblings in my grandmother's family, after all. Sometimes I didn't understand what The Story was about, but I laughed anyway just for the sheer joy of sharing in the happiness of the family. I would sit in my dad's lap or sometimes on the floor at the foot of some uncle or aunt's feet, gazing up in pure adoration at all of them; I thought they were all magical in some way.

There were prerequisites for telling The Story, too: There was usually a lot of drinking—we were an Irish family that definitely perpetuated the stereotype. In retrospect, that could be why the volume went up... As a kid, though, all I saw were the smiles, the jokes, and the hugs that always happened when we were all together. There was also the required singing. Every person in my grandmother's family had a repertoire of at least ten Irish songs solidly memorized. Great-Aunt Katherine had a deep, alto voice, and she was proud of her ability to harmonize. Her twin, Uncle Buddy, always quipped that she sounded just like him, which would set off a series of short-lived arguments that eventually resolved with laughter. And of course, there was the food. Endless food, but always marmalade and raisin toast for Nana's breakfast with whiskey as an hors d'oeuvre at five. Nana, my great-grandmother, was a tiny woman who wore black, thick-heeled sensible shoes and a ribbon hairband in her snowy hair. She wasn't very sensible about everything, though; the family often chided her about the one cigarette she would sneak in the bathroom each day or the one glass of sherry she would imbibe each night. It added to their story hour.

Not everyone from my grandmother's family attended all the gatherings. Several members of the family were scattered around the West Coast, but the majority lived up and down the eastern coastline. It was rare to see all of them together, but it didn't matter who came; the stories lived on through the voices of those who were there.

When I was ten, my family was invited to a reunion at my Great-Aunt Joan's in Springfield, Massachusetts. That meant meeting lots of cousins, swimming in the lake nearby, and sleeping on cots in the barn. Would I see Great-Aunt Joan in her blue bra again? That was the only image I had of her from a visit to our house in Virginia. She had shamelessly stripped down in the midst of family, claiming that the Virginia heat was too oppressive. I was quickly whisked out of the room, my mouth agape but oh, so interested. I would also get to meet my Great-Uncle Malcolm for the first time. Malcolm was the Handsome One, according to my mother. His wife, Ida, and their two girls would be coming with him from Idaho. I couldn't wait!

The first two days in Springfield were glorious; I was in seventh heaven. My cousins and I were partners in crime; there were no adults checking on us in the barn to see how late it was before we fell asleep. They were too busy telling stories by the fire pit on the back deck to notice us. Late afternoon on the third day, the family gathered for dinner outside on makeshift tables. The cousins and I made a beeline for the dessert table before one of the adults shooed us toward the grill for hamburgers and hot dogs. We sat and ate in the grass and didn't worry about the mustard or ketchup that spilled on our clothes. Life was good. I glanced up from a mouthful of hamburger to see my cousin Diane, who was nineteen and gorgeous, run into the house crying hysterically. I was immediately worried because I idolized her. She actually talked to me and treated me like I was her equal. What was wrong?

Everyone got very quiet. Great-Uncle Malcolm walked to the center of a grassy spot amidst the family, holding a beer and smiling. But the rest of the family was not smiling. In fact, many of them were crying, too. I remember my dad had his arm around my mom, who had buried her face in his shirt. Great-Aunt Joan sitting tall and proud on the steps with tears streaming down her face; Great-Aunt Gloria sobbing loudly. Then he sang. I realized then that Malcolm was not only The Handsome One but also The One with the Golden Voice. His voice rang strong, clear, and true. Mournful, soulful words from the family repertoire—"the pipes, the pipes are calling." I recognized the song—it was the classic, "Danny Boy." Time slowed. I smelled the grass near my feet; I heard a lawn mower somewhere down the street; I heard the cries of the Storytellers who had formed a protective circle around their Malcolm. The entire place was quiet. The cousins stopped talking. We were mesmerized. The song reverberated in our brains. I had never heard it sung like that before, and I had heard it many times. Why? I didn't understand.

The last lines of the song told the story: "I shall sleep in peace until you come to me..." The song ended, but the words did not. Malcom's wife walked to him in the middle of the grass, in the middle of the circle, toward him in the middle of his life. Even as a kid, I knew something was terribly wrong. No one had told me. This was a *different* story. Malcolm died a year later from his battle with leukemia. He didn't know it, but he had stirred a story inside my heart at the tender age of ten.